FIGHTING
FAKE NEWS!

FIGHTING FAKE NEWS!

Teaching Critical Thinking and Media Literacy in a Digital Age

Brian C. Housand, Ph.D.

PRUFROCK PRESS INC.

WACO, TEXAS

Prufrock Press Inc.
P.O. Box 8813
Waco, TX 76714-8813
Phone: (800) 998-2208
Fax: (800) 240-0333
http://www.prufrock.com

TABLE OF CONTENTS

ACTIVITY GUIDE

CHAPTER 1

THE WORLD OF
FAKE NEWS:
HOW DID WE GET HERE?

It is said that there is an ancient Chinese curse: *May you live in interesting times.* As we consider the world that we are living in today and all that is happening around us, we are definitely living in *interesting* times. We are constantly bombarded with a deluge of news and information through an ever-increasing variety of technology outlets. From radio and television, to computers and mobile devices, we are seldom, if ever, truly unplugged from the technology and media that surround us.

Today's technology has given us unprecedented access to information and equipped us with powerful tools for creativity and communication. Yet, we must ask the question, "At what cost?" As technology advances and becomes more personalized, do we sacrifice our privacy for the sake of the future? Do we blindly trust in our tools and online resources to provide us with the most relevant and up-to-date information possible? At what point do we begin to question what we are reading online?

As we consider this "ancient Chinese curse," we should also begin speculating about its origin and authenticity. In the digital age, each of us carries a powerful tool for locating information. A quick Google search immediately casts a long shadow of a doubt on the origin of this phrase that many have simply taken for granted for decades. Despite making its way into numerous speeches delivered by the likes of Albert Camus, Arthur C. Clarke, and Robert F. Kennedy, there is no solid evidence that this is even of Chinese origin—let alone an ancient curse.

Yet, why have we willingly accepted this quotation as fact? Do we believe it because it fits our schema, or do we believe it simply because we want to believe it is true? Maybe we believe it because it makes an interesting story, or are we willing to believe anything that we read?

I warn you of this ancient Chinese curse because we have always and will always live in interesting times. The interesting times of today are not necessarily that different than the interesting times of yesterday or even 100 years ago. We are all too quick to revel in the "good old days" without admitting that they were probably not as "good" as we remember them. Today's times may seem more interesting and even dire because we are currently experiencing them, or perhaps they seem more interesting because we are beginning to pay attention to what is happening around us.

A BRIEF HISTORY OF FAKE NEWS

As we look at our world today, we hear the constant cry of fake news. Claims come from our social media feeds, 24-hour cable news channels, and even the Trump White House. The rise of such claims and alternative facts during the 2016 presidential election led to *post-truth* being proclaimed as the 2016 Oxford Dictionaries Word of the Year. The term is defined as "relating to or denoting circumstances in which objective facts are less influential in shaping public opinion than appeals to emotion and personal belief." With 2016 events such as the Brexit vote and the U.S. presidential election, use of the term increased by approximately 2,000% more than its usage in 2015.

As we have always lived in interesting times, the concept of fake news has been around a lot longer than we may have realized.

In a *2016 POLITICO Magazine* article, Jacob Soll related "The Long and Brutal History of Fake News" and advised us that, "Bogus news has been around a lot longer than real news. And it's left a lot of destruction behind" (para. 1). According to Soll, fake news began circulating with the introduction of the Guttenberg Press in 1439. News sources of the time ranged from religious authorities and political organizations to supposed eyewitness accounts of sailors and merchants. Yet, there were no standards for journalistic integrity or ethical behavior. Instead, readers had to pay close attention and determine what the real story might be. Because the technology of the day was in the hands of a few, a great deal of value was placed in what was printed.

As printing technology expanded over the next 300 years, so did fake news. By the mid-1700s, "newsworthy" accounts of sea monsters and witches abounded. There were numerous reports by churches and European authorities blaming sinners for natural disasters, including the 1755 earthquake in Lisbon, Portugal. These claims prompted Voltaire to advocate against fake religious news.

Meanwhile in the American Colonies, Soll (2016) pointed out that even our Founding Fathers were perpetrators of fake news for political advantage, as Benjamin Franklin "concocted propaganda stories about murderous 'scalping'

Indians working in league with the British King George III" (para. 10). It was fake news stories such as these that helped to compel colonists to enlist to fight in the Revolutionary War.

Throughout history, fake news has proved to be financially rewarding for its publishers. In the 1830s, there was a rise in popularity of "penny press" newspapers that cost only one cent and featured a narrative style of reporting that attracted a wider audience than more traditional newspapers. In August of 1835, *The Sun*, a New York newspaper, published a series of stories over 6 days that reported that well-known British astronomer Sir John Herschel had constructed a powerful telescope that allowed him to view life on the moon. The paper provided extensively detailed descriptions and illustrations of the vegetation and animals, including single-horned goats and beavers that for some reason walked on two feet. There were also descriptions of human-like creatures with wings and pyramid structures that formed this advanced civilization. As a result of these fantastical stories, sales and subscriptions flourished. Although many competing newspapers were quick to point out that this was mere fantasy, other newspapers around the world reprinted the stories as fact. *The Sun* never admitted that the stories were fake news, but instead, the Great Moon Hoax helped it become a successful newspaper.

By the late 1800s, the American public saw the rise of yellow journalism. This was a style of newspaper reporting that emphasized sensationalism rather than factual information. Ironically, one of the greatest purveyors of the surge of yellow journalism was Joseph Pulitzer, for whom the Pulitzer Prize, an award recognizing excellence in newspaper journalism, is named. To increase sales and circulation of *The New York World*, editor Pulitzer published sensationalized news stories that emphasized crime, disasters, and scandal. In 1895, William Randolph Hearst purchased the *New York Morning Journal* and began a head-to-head competition with Pulitzer for the greatest circulation. Many believe that Hearst's sensationalized accounts of Spanish atrocities in Cuba helped start the Spanish-American War. According to Soll (2016), "When Hearst's correspondent in Havana wired that there would be no war, Hearst famously responded: 'You furnish the pictures, I'll furnish the war'" (para. 12).

As technology continued to develop in the 20th century, we began get our news from the radio, and just like what was reported as news in print was blindly accepted, the same seemed to ring true on the radio. On Sunday, October 30, 1938, The Mercury Theater on the Air broadcast the now infamous radio play adaptation of H. G. Wells's novel *The War of the Worlds*. Directed and narrated by Orson Welles, the program simulated a live news broadcast in which New Jersey and New York were under attack by space aliens. Since its original airing, it has been accepted as fact that this single broadcast caused mass hysteria and struck fear into the hearts of the nation. It has been widely reported and believed that listeners panicked thinking that the Earth was actually under attack by invaders from Mars.

However, this was not what actually happened. Since that time, much speculation has been cast as to the actual number of listeners to the program. According to a telephone survey of 5,000 individuals, only 2% reported that they were listening to the radio program on the night of October 30, 1938. Instead, much of the hype and hysteria was created by the newspaper headlines the following morning. The cover of the October 31, 1938, *New York Daily News* proclaimed, "FAKE RADIO 'WAR' STIRS TERROR THROUGH U.S." (see Figure 1), and despite the radio program not even airing in Boston, the headline of *The Boston Daily Globe* read "RADIO PLAY TERRIFIES NATION." The newspaper stories reported mass hysteria and that many feared that the world was coming to an end.

Despite the news stories, there is little evidence to suggest that any of this actually occurred. Instead, it is now believed that the newspapers were all too quick to criticize the unreliability of radio to accurately report news. Newspapers were fearful that they were losing their customers to the new medium. In a sense, newspapers were printing fake news in an attempt to discourage the public from believing what they heard on the radio.

This fight for the public's attention was confounded even further with the advent of the television. The major networks enjoyed little competition for viewers' attention from the 1950s through the 1970s. Yet, that all changed on June 1, 1980, when Ted Turner launched CNN as the first cable news channel. What had once been a 30-minute nightly broadcast of national news suddenly transformed into a 24-hour-a-day need for news. This went on to inspire multiple other cable news channels, including Fox News and MSNBC. As a result of multiple news stations that are always on, these channels have had to devise ways to fill their time with sensationalized stories and political commentary designed to entertain and engage viewers perhaps more than simply reporting the news.

Today, the sensationalism and yellow journalism of the late 19th century is alive and well in supermarket tabloids like the *National Enquirer*, whose scintillating headlines featuring celebrity scandals serve as distractors from the drudgery of our daily lives. The unbelievable and often ridiculous *World Weekly News*, published from 1979 to 2007, featured fake news stories, such as Bat Boy, the existence of aliens, and Elvis being alive, but its news stories were not much different than the clickbait that is scattered across many of today's websites.

According to a 2016 Pew Research Center study, 62% of U.S. adults reported getting their news on social media. In the survey of 4,654 members of the Pew Research Center's American Trends panel, researchers found that users of Reddit, Facebook, and Twitter were most likely to get news from each of these sites compared to other social media platforms. Two-thirds of Facebook users (66%) and 59% of Twitter users reported getting news from these sites. Meanwhile, 70% of Reddit users are getting their news from that site. Other social media platforms were reported as being used by less than 25% of the respondents.

In a 2017 study from Common Sense Media (Robb, 2017), 853 children ages 10–18 were asked how they got news from each source "yesterday." Figure 2 shows the results in graph format.

As kids get older, they are more likely to utilize social networking sites to get their news. Only 20% of "tweens," or kids ages 10–12 years old, reported getting news from social networking sites, while 47% of teens ages 13–18 did (Robb, 2017).

Figure 1. Fake news in headlines.

Although these numbers are may not be cause of concern by themselves, it is somewhat worrisome that 64% of those surveyed indicated that they only get news from one social networking site, with the most common response being Facebook. Only 26% reported getting their news from two or more sites, and alarmingly only 10% get their news on three or more sites.

These data are indicative of the great migration from traditional news sources to online and social media sources that has transpired since the turn of the century. In the age of the Internet, news and media agencies are on the same playing field

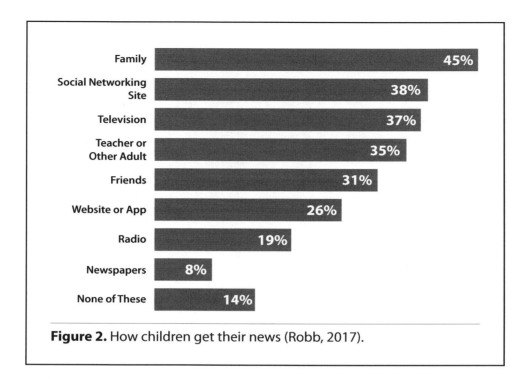

Figure 2. How children get their news (Robb, 2017).

with almost any individual or small group of individuals with a moderate amount of web design skills.

Indeed, these are *interesting* times. As Soll (2016) concluded:

> Real news is not coming back in any tangible way on a competitive local level, or as a driver of opinion in a world where the majority of the population does not rely on professionally reported news sources and so much news is filtered via social media, and by governments. And as real news recedes, fake news will grow. We've seen the terrifying results this has had in the past—and our biggest challenge will be to find a new way to combat the rising tide. (para. 18)

THE PURPOSE OF THIS BOOK

To combat this rising tide of fake news and alternative facts, we must first become and then teach our students to become more critical consumers of the information that they encounter. However, like fake news, this idea is nothing new. Our librarians and media specialists have been telling us this probably for as long as there have been libraries. They have advised us to use multiple sources and to read critically when gathering information. Scientists have cast heavy doses of skepticism in their attempts to discover truth. Researchers have long called for increased rigor in data collection and analysis while pursuing statistical significance in their findings. Although none of this is new, it has perhaps become more urgent to develop these types of skills at a younger age and, perhaps more importantly, use these skills throughout one's lifetime.

As we have already pointed out, access to information through the Internet and various digital devices serve to both expand our access and to complicate matters completely. As we consider what we can do as educators to better prepare our students for the world of today, we will examine four challenges that confront us in the digital age and propose a series of activities to overcome these challenges.

Challenge One: Information Overload

With access to an almost infinite amount of information at our fingertips, it is all too easy to feel overwhelmed by the amount of information that is available, but is this a new problem? Just as we have seen in the long history of fake news, feelings of information overload have been present in every generation. In 1970, Alvin Toffler described this psychological state as "future shock." Indeed, the world as we know it has changed greatly since 1970, but for those living then, they were *interesting* times. In order to be successful in today's time, students must be able to successfully navigate the Internet and locate the information they are searching for. Although our information gathering was once limited by our access to physical libraries and the quality and quantity of their resources, we now have access to vast amounts of online resources through the digital devices that we carry with us. New York University new media professor Clay Shirky (2008) claimed the challenge may not be having access to too much information, instead redefining the challenge as filter failure. We have to be able to determine which information we actually need. For our students, this may be even more difficult to determine.

Challenge Two: The Crisis of Authenticity

Although it is wonderful that today's technology tools allow anyone to easily create content and share it with the world, we also need to be aware that this allows anyone to create and share anything that they want with the same power and authority as the news media, organizations, and experts in the field. On the surface, there may be very little to distinguish between a reputable source and a dubious one. To overcome the crisis of authenticity, we must empower our students to employ a variety of strategies to uncover the reliability and trustworthiness of the information that they encounter on a daily basis.

Challenge Three: Speed Versus Accuracy

In the age of Google, we often equate being smart with how quickly we can locate information with our digital devices. Speed of recall has always been celebrated as a sign of intelligence, but as Benjamin Bloom and colleagues (1956) pointed out with his taxonomy of cognitive thinking, recall or remembering serves as the lowest level of thinking. If we only focus on how quickly students are able to retrieve the answer, then we may be unknowingly sacrificing accuracy in the name of speed. That being said, we should not only focus on finding the "right" answer, but also on encouraging our students to meaningfully apply and utilize information for creative productivity.

Challenge Four: Overcoming Our Own Bias

As technology and social media have advanced, they have allowed for a more personalized experience. Our every move online is being tracked, and advertisements are being customized for us based on our search history and sites that we frequent. By connecting with other like-minded people through Twitter or Facebook, we are building valuable social capital, but we need to also be aware that we may be unknowingly putting ourselves into an information bubble. Inside of this echo chamber, we encounter only information that we may agree with and little information that contradicts our beliefs, even if those beliefs are mistaken. We must work with our students to help them identify their own biases and to expand their ways of thinking in a search for truth.

FIGHTING FAKE NEWS!

To overcome these four challenges and to empower students to fight fake news, a series of activities have been devised for this book. These activities are grounded by theory based on the New Literacies framework, which will be described in the following chapter. The activities are not meant to be exhaustive, but instead represent the first steps toward developing critical thinking skills in students in digital environments. There are three levels for utilizing the activities:

1. **Teacher uses one of the activities in the book.** This is the entry-level approach. When selecting an activity, determine whether or not it will meet the needs of your students. Identify the purpose and objective for introducing the activity. Not all of the activities will necessarily meet the needs of all of your students. Also, the activities and resources are not necessarily sequential.

2. **Teacher creates a new activity based on an idea from the book.** Consider ways to meaningfully adapt an existing activity for your students. It may be helpful to use an activity as described in the book first, and then devise modifications to best fit with the needs of your students. Finding existing

curriculum and remixing it for your own purposes and needs is just good teaching. Look for ways to make this work best for you.

3. **Students create new activities based on an idea from the book.** The activities in this book are meant to be beginnings and not ending points. Just as you are encouraged to adapt lessons for your own needs, I also encourage you to challenge your students to adapt the activities for themselves. The real power of learning comes when we help transition students to levels of creativity. To scaffold this transition, each section of the book contains at least one activity designed to move students *from consumers to producers.*

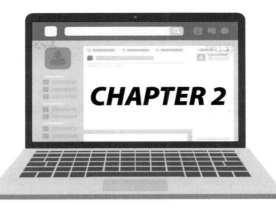

CHAPTER 2

A NEW LITERACIES FRAMEWORK

The year was 2006. I was in the first year of my Ph.D. program, and although I originally came to the University of Connecticut for gifted education, my interests were expanding into the direction of technology. Those were interesting and exciting times—YouTube had just been invented the year prior, Facebook was only open to those who had university e-mail addresses, and being lucky enough to have a Gmail address was a sign of tech savviness. In 2006, we were still a year away from the introduction of the iPhone, and access to the Internet, especially Wi-Fi, was more of a privilege than what has today become a basic expectation of a civilized society.

It was in 2006 that Don Leu and the New Literacies Research Team at the University of Connecticut first cast a harsh light on the rapidly changing world of reading in online environments. By now, we have all heard the story. A group of advanced middle school readers were asked what it meant for something to be reliable. Of course, they were all able to define this term. They were then asked to locate information about the Pacific Northwest Tree Octopus. Of course, they were all able to use a number of different Internet browsers, search engines, and search terms and successfully locate the website *Save the Pacific Northwest Tree Octopus* at http://zapatopi.net/treeoctopus (see Figure 3), but what happened next was a shock to the system.

When asked if the information that they found on the website satisfied their definition of "reliable," with little to no exception, all of these top readers said, "Yes."

It seemed that all logic, reason, and knowledge of octopi and other cephalopods being marine-based animals with gills was completely thrown to the wind.

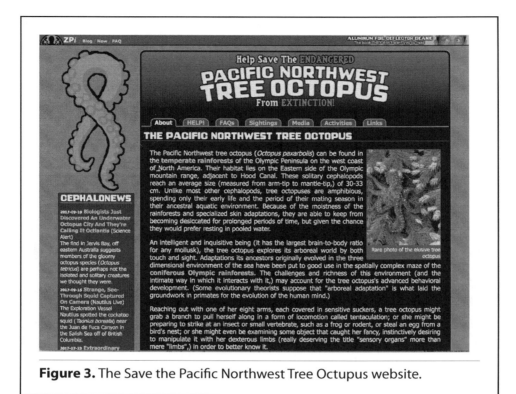

Figure 3. The Save the Pacific Northwest Tree Octopus website.

Students were easily fooled by what has become perhaps one of the most well-known Internet hoaxes of all time simply because there was a photo of an octopus in a tree on a website that used the standard conventions of the day. Perhaps others were distracted by the scientific name included, *octopus paxarbolis* (which, by the way, is not a real thing). Perhaps it was the links to actual news stories or even that the page features an awareness ribbon in the shape of a tentacle. Whatever the reason, this site designed in 1998 by Lyle Zapato had successfully duped a group of advanced middle school students. Based on these findings, Leu declared that even the brightest students in 2006 were woefully unprepared to determine whether or not the Pacific Northwest Tree Octopus was an Internet hoax.

At that point, rather than focusing our attention on teaching students to be more critical consumers of the information they encounter, many educators chose to wage an all-out war on Wikipedia. Many teachers and librarians were outraged at the mere idea of an online encyclopedia that anyone could edit. Yet more than a decade later, many would argue that Wikipedia is often a more credible source than a set of encyclopedias sitting on a library's shelf. Instead of blaming Wikipedia and other Internet resources, we should have directed our attention to teaching students to develop a set of New Literacies that would guide them in an information age. To accomplish, this Leu and his team (Leu et al., 2007) established a New

Literacies framework comprised of five essential skills needed by students to be successful in online environments:

1. Identifying Important Questions
2. Locating Information
3. Critically Evaluating Information
4. Synthesizing Information
5. Communicating Information

IDENTIFYING IMPORTANT QUESTIONS

Unlike in more traditional reading environments, when we utilize the Internet, we are typically guided by a question, a problem, or a need for information. Despite the name Internet browser, we are seldom "browsing." Instead, we are much more likely to be actively "searching." Taboada and Guthrie (2006) suggested that reading initiated by a question or problem differs in important ways from reading that does not. Quite simply, when reading is guided by an initial question or need for information, readers are more engaged in the process. Put another way, beginning with the end in mind helps to direct readers toward the information that is desired or needed.

LOCATING INFORMATION

After students have identified the question to be answered, they then begin to locate information using the Internet. To be successful in this endeavor, one must (1) know how to use a search engine by composing a set of search terms; (2) read and decipher the search engine results before selecting a page to visit; (3) once on a webpage, locate information that might be present there; and (4) make inferences about where additional information might be located by following a link on one page to find information on another page or even a separate site. When we compare this type of reading to more traditional reading instruction, this is significantly more complex. Even if we provide students with a single URL to visit for the information, they may find themselves venturing off in myriad directions as they locate additional information.

CRITICALLY EVALUATING INFORMATION

Once students have successfully located information on the Internet, they must then critically evaluate the information. This presents a unique set of challenges in comparison to more traditional reading environments. Coiro (2007) has found at least five different types of evaluation that occur during online reading comprehension:

1. Evaluating understanding: Does it make sense to me?
2. Evaluating relevancy: Does it meet my needs?
3. Evaluating accuracy: Can I verify it with another reliable source?
4. Evaluating reliability: Can I trust it?
5. Evaluating bias: How does the author shape it?

To assist students in evaluating information, we must teach them the skills necessary to do so. As we have already seen with the tree octopus and with the rampant nature of fake news that is now prevalent, development of these skills is critical.

SYNTHESIZING INFORMATION

Since the introduction of the original Bloom's taxonomy, synthesis has been the hallmark of higher order thinking. With the revised taxonomy of skills at the turn of the 21st century, synthesis was replaced by the verb *create*. Although I am all for promoting creativity in our students, I think that we may have mistakenly lost something essential to critical thinking with the removal of synthesis from the taxonomy. Perhaps synthesis was replaced because it is so challenging to observe, as it happens quickly and takes place in the minds of our students. In this sense, how synthesis occurs is something of a mystery. Because readers are actively constructing the texts they read based on the links that they follow, no two readers will necessarily have the same online reading experience.

COMMUNICATING INFORMATION

After students have synthesized the information, they are then tasked with communicating information using an ever-increasing number of digital tools and platforms. Each tool has its own set of affordances, and each requires a different set of skills and strategies for use. As we consider the plethora of digital ecosystems available to us, it is a rather daunting task to take on when trying to teach our students how to successfully navigate each of these environments. Rather than tackling each tool individually, we must instead acknowledge that technology is constantly changing and work with our students to develop practical, common-sense approaches to using a variety of tools.

With the five stages of the New Literacies framework in mind, we will next explore specific strategies and activities for actively engaging our students and developing their critical thinking skills in digital environments. Each of the next five chapters focuses on one of the stages of the New Literacies framework. In each chapter, I will provide a collection of activities for you to use with your students. The activities are not necessarily intended to be used sequentially. Instead, the hope is that you will consider the needs of your students and select activities that are appropriate to their needs. Each chapter also features a From Consumer to Producer section. Although I believe that there is a great deal of value in completing the activities as they are presented, there is perhaps even more that can be learned from students adapting the existing activities to create their own examples.

IDENTIFYING IMPORTANT QUESTIONS

Think back to when you first met the Internet. At that time, we were living in the age of dial-up connections, which by today's standards seems like the Dark Ages. When the Age of the Internet began, we were dependent on services like America Online to provide content for us. As Internet connection speeds increased, we saw the rise of the Internet browser. In the late 1990s, services like Yahoo! reigned supreme. During this time we were rather passive as we played the part of browsing through online content. Consider the screenshot of what Yahoo! looked like in July of 1997 (see Figure 4).

Here we were presented with a collection of categorical links to click on for more information. To best navigate this digital environment, we would work our way through the levels until we found the site that we were actually looking for. In many ways, using Yahoo! was reminiscent of browsing the shelves in a large library. We would find the section, the row, the shelf, and finally the book. Although Yahoo! did possess a search box, few people ever seemed to make use of this tool.

With the introduction of Google, everything changed. I can remember very vividly seeing Google for the first time in early 2000 and being startled by what was on the page—or rather, by what was not on the page. Instead of all of the familiar categories of Yahoo!, Google essentially offered a blank page with a search box and two buttons: The first, "Google Search," and the second, "I'm Feeling Lucky," which almost seemed to be daring you to click on it (see Figure 5). To be quite honest, I thought that something must be wrong with my Internet connection. This could not possibly be the correct site.

I wondered aloud, "You mean I have to type something in that box? Where is my content?" and it was in this very moment that I, like many other Internet users,

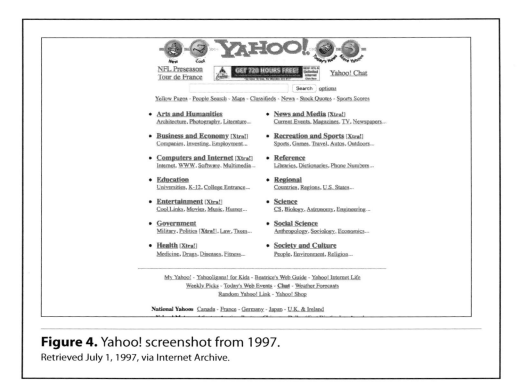

Figure 4. Yahoo! screenshot from 1997.

Retrieved July 1, 1997, via Internet Archive.

Figure 5. Google screenshot from 2000.

Google and the Google logo are registered trademarks of Google Inc., used with permission.
Retrieved February 29, 2000, via Internet Archive.

went from being a passive browser of information to being an active searcher. For the first time, users had to figure out what they looking for. We had to have a question or a purpose for searching. In an instant, we had access to an almost infinite amount of information, and all we had to do was be able to compose a search term.

Yet, today in many ways the pendulum has swung back from active searching to passive consumerism. Although we still have the power to utilize search engines for the information that we seek, much of the information that we are confronted with comes to us via social media outlets like Facebook, Twitter, and Reddit. We will look at ways to better navigate those environments in Chapter 7: Communicating Information. In the meantime, let's examine some ways that we can best help students to use the powerful search engines of today.

CONSTRUCTING BETTER SEARCH TERMS

When using an Internet search engine, we are often in search of the solution to a problem or the answer to question that is puzzling us. Alternately, we might be looking for more information on a topic of interest. Regardless, we must work with our students to help them learn how to identify important questions and begin their searches with the end in mind.

Although we use most likely use search engines like Google and Bing on a daily basis, have you ever stopped to consider how you learned to use these tools or better yet, how your students learn to use these tools? We almost take for granted that our students will have a basic understanding of how to conduct a search because they have always had access to the Internet. However, I would challenge you to spend a little time giving your students a search task and taking time to observe how they go about constructing a set of search terms.

Many students may phrase their search in the form of a question. Although it is becoming more and more common to simply use Siri or Alexa for this type of information, the most relevant search results may not be returned. Therefore, you should share some of the following tips with your students to help make them more savvy searchers.

Identify the Key Terms

Rather than phrasing your search as a question, try to identify all of the key terms in your question. Work to eliminate any common words or phrases that might produce undesired results. Instead choose words that are as specific as possible. As an activity for your students, pose several questions for them and have them identify the search terms that they would use without using the Internet. This will help them to focus on composing better search terms rather then becoming distracted by millions of search results.

Order Matters

Although search engines do examine each word separately, the order of the words in a search does matter. Consider the difference in results when searching for *blue sky* versus the results produced for *sky blue*.

Every Word Matters

Try searching for *who* versus *the who* versus *a who*. The first produces results about the World Health Organization and the pronoun. The second provides a list of results about the English rock band, The Who. The third gives us results focused on the Dr. Seuss creation *Horton Hears a Who!* This example shows how even an article such as "the" or "a" can significantly alter the search results.

Capitalization Does Not Matter

On the other hand, whether words are capitalized or not does not affect the search results. Try searching for *Albert Einstein* and *albert einstein*. The same set of results will be returned.

Use "Quotation Marks" for Exact Phrases

Often you will want to search for information that contains an exact phrase. This is especially useful when looking for a direct quote. When quotation marks are used in a search, then the exact phase will be searched.

Wildcards

Putting a * in your word or phrase will serve as a wildcard. For example try searching for the phrase *"largest * in the world."* This will produce a large list of results that may prompt students' curiosity about topics that they may not have thought of otherwise. For example, my search using *"largest * in the world"* led me to sites about the largest cities, countries, animals, trees, shopping malls, airports, and islands. Just be aware that this type of searching may result in some unexpected Internet rabbit holes for your students, prompting them to say things like, "I didn't know I was interested in that."

The Minus Sign

Using a - or the minus sign can eliminate what Google refers to as "invasive results" from the results page. Note that there should not a space between the minus sign and the term that is being removed. Including a space will not produce the same results.

For example, you might search for *salsa* and be confronted with more than 250,000,000 results. If you are looking for a salsa recipe you might try searching using the terms *salsa -dancing -music*. This produces 68,000,000 results focused primarily on recipes for salsa. Alternatively, if you are allergic to tomatoes you could try searching for *salsa recipe -tomato* to find a better set of results.

Combine Searches With OR

Although the minus sign eliminates part of the search results, the use of OR between searches combines searches together. OR must be in uppercase letters for this trick to work. This works especially well when combining terms in quotation marks together.

Define:

Although a simple search for word may automatically produce a definition, that is not always the case. To force Google to provide a definition, include *define:* before the search. For example, compare the results for *astronomy* and *define: astronomy*. The latter produces a dictionary box at the top of the results (see Figure 6).

Be certain to click the light gray downward-pointing arrow to reveal translations, word origin, and more definitions.

Search on a Specific Site

Although many websites do feature a search box allowing you to search the contents of only their website, Google offers the ability to do this for any website. Simply put *site:* in front of a site or domain and then enter your search terms. For example, if you were looking for information about the Mars Rover Curiosity on the NASA website, you could use the search terms *site:nasa.gov curiosity*. This will restrict the results to only those found on the nasa.gov website.

Advanced Search

Beyond the basic search, Google also offers a set of advanced search tools that can be accessed at https://www.google.com/advanced_search. Many of the strategies mentioned in this section are able to be performed within a scaffolded environment for beginning searchers. This can help your students better realize how to use quotation marks to find exact words or phrases, look for any of these words by typing OR between all of the words that you want to include, or by using the minus sign just before words that you do not want to include. In addition, the Google

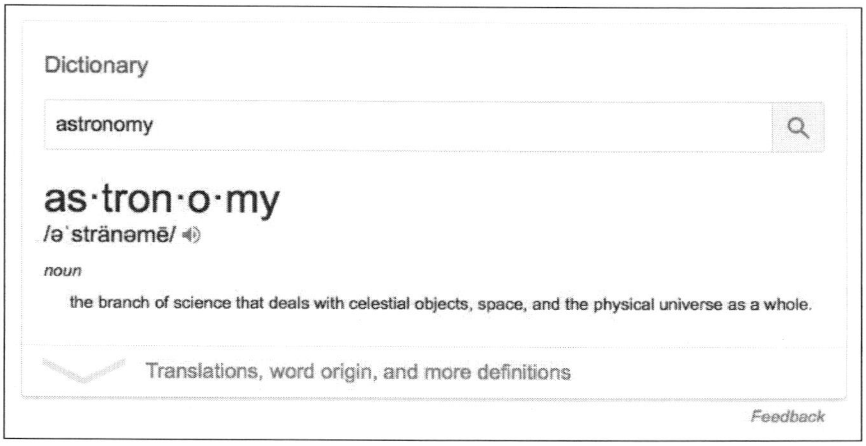

Figure 6. Google define: sample result.
Google and the Google logo are registered trademarks of Google Inc., used with permission.

Advanced Search page allows you to search for numbers existing between a specified range.

Advanced Search can also narrow the results by language, geographical region, site or domain, and file type. Particularly useful when looking for the most recent and up-to-date information, a search can also be conducted for information updated in the past 24 hours, past week, past month, or past year.

From Consumer to Producer

After introducing or reviewing these search tips with your students, try providing them with some intriguing questions to answer. However, rather than simply turning them loose on the Internet, have them compose a set of search terms that they believe would provide the best results. Once your students have constructed their search terms, have them put their creations to the test.

Although it is perfectly acceptable for you to present your students with a set of questions, we want to encourage your students to move from consumers to producers. Instead, have your students design a set of intriguing questions for their classmates to construct search terms for. As part of this process, the students designing the questions should identify what they consider to be an appropriate response for a set of search terms. Then have another student try out her newly developed skills for identifying important questions and constructing search terms without and then with a web search engine.

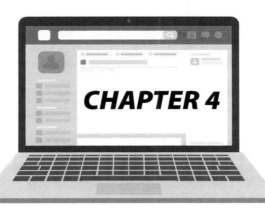

CHAPTER 4

LOCATING INFORMATION

Now that you and your students have identified important questions to be answered, it is time to focus on locating information to answer those questions. As we saw in the last chapter, there is a great deal to consider when composing a set of search terms. After entering those terms into a search engine, things begin to get really interesting—as millions of results are returned in less than a second. The question then becomes, "Where do I begin?" If you have spent any amount of time watching your students search, you have undoubtedly witnessed them systematically clicking through the links in the order that they appear on the page. As you have gained more practice with locating information, you have probably realized that the first link is not always the best link to satisfy your need for information.

In this chapter, we will explore two activities designed to help your students sharpen their skills of locating information.

ONE CLICK

Undoubtedly, we have all heard the advice to "look before you leap." When searching for information online, this moral is also advisable. When confronted with page after page of search results, the natural temptation would be to click on the first one. Instead, we should advise our students to "look before they click" and decode the information that is contained in the search results.

For example, if one were searching for the name of Blackbeard's pirate ship, one might use the search terms *Blackbeard pirate ship* and find about 481,000 results.

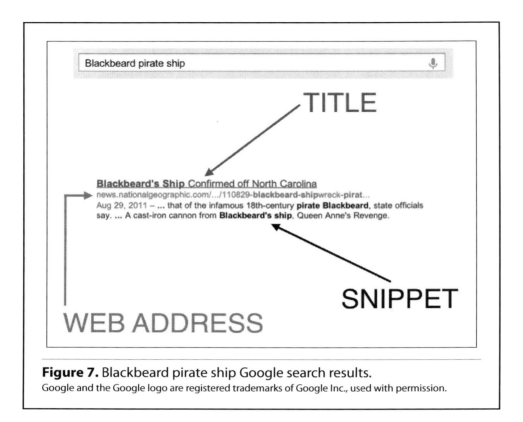

Figure 7. Blackbeard pirate ship Google search results.
Google and the Google logo are registered trademarks of Google Inc., used with permission.

In glancing through the results, the information in Figure 7 appears near the top of the list.

By examining the web address (which is highlighted in green), we see that the information is located at https://news.nationalgeographic.com. This indicates that this information is coming from the news section on the *National Geographic* website. Given the source, it is highly likely that this information is trustworthy. Because this is a news item, the date that it was published on the Internet is also included. We see that the story is from August 29, 2011. The title of the website is indicated by a blue hyperlink. From this, we learn that the location of the ship was confirmed off of the coast of North Carolina. We should also note that our search terms *Blackbeard pirate ship* all appear in a **bold** font. Finally, by reading the snippet or brief summary of key text that appears, you will learn that the name of the ship is *Queen Anne's Revenge*.

By teaching students the anatomy of search results, they will have a better idea of what information they might find on a website before clicking on a list of search results. To guide them in this process, introduce them to the One Click activity. Start by providing them with the list of search results for *superman comic* in Activity 1 at the end of this chapter (p. 32). Then provide them with the list of questions also found at the end of this chapter on pages 33–34. (Note that for ease of use, all of the handouts for the activities I mention in this book can be found at the end of each chapter.)

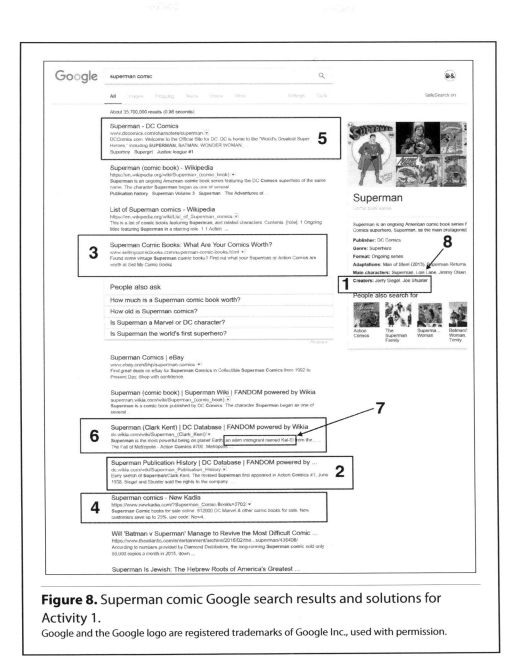

Figure 8. Superman comic Google search results and solutions for Activity 1.
Google and the Google logo are registered trademarks of Google Inc., used with permission.

Although there may be multiple answers to any of these questions, Figure 8 shows some possible solutions.

From Consumer to Producer

The One Click activity could be done with any topic or search, and I suggest that you create your own based on topics that you might be studying in class or, better yet, on the interests of the students. In using this activity with students, I have found that it often works better to provide them with a printed page of the search results. This forces them to be critical of the information that is on the page instead of just clicking on links on the Internet.

To help students move from consumer to producer, challenge students to create their own One Click activity for others to solve. By having them create their own, they are forced to closely review the results on a page and to devise a series of questions that go along with the information that is provided.

To help get your students started, begin with the results for a search of the word *Mars* on page 35. Have your students devise 5–8 possible questions based on these search results. You can see how the results presented in the handout were guided by the news of the day and an announcement made by Elon Musk. Also, a search for Mars returned a link to the musical artist Bruno Mars. This makes for a good distractor in the results. Depending on what information you might be looking for, looking before you click can save you valuable time.

Next, challenge your students to develop their own One Click activities based on topics of their interests. They should develop 5–8 questions to accompany their search results. Because search results are constantly changing, have students print their search results or save them as a PDF. This will ensure that the results remain constant and match the questions that they have created. Next, have students highlight where the answers to each of their questions can be located. Then have them exchange their One Click activities with their classmates. This will allow them to practice the skill of locating information and also learn about the interests of their peers.

MULTISTEP SEARCH PROBLEMS

As a former elementary school teacher, one of the things that often puzzled my students was learning how to solve multistep math problems. Although they could easily solve problems that involved a single step, when they had to use information from one problem to solve another, even some of my brightest students struggled in the beginning. Locating information online is really no different. Many will be able to easily locate information using a single search, but when confronted with a question that requires multiple searches or using information learned from one search to guide another search, many may lose their way before finding the answer that they are looking for. To better prepare students to more quickly and efficiently find information, let's challenge them by asking interest-based questions that may require multiple searches to find the answer. Sometimes multistep search problems may come in the form of a single question, but more often than not, these problems are comprised of a series of related questions. Take for example this set of questions:

- Who or what was on the first U.S. postage stamp?
- How much did it cost?
- In what year was it issued?

Although you could easily ask the first question, it seems only natural to follow up with the other two questions to help students delve a bit deeper beyond the "one" right answer. By asking relevant follow-up questions, it also potentially forces a deeper examination of the information that they may find online. This set of questions regarding the first U.S. postage stamp is interesting and intentionally confusing for students because they will find that two stamps were issued at the same time in 1847. One stamp cost 10 cents and featured an image of George Washington, and the other stamp portrayed Benjamin Franklin and cost only 5 cents.

At this point, students may become frustrated that there are seemingly two correct answers. Some may try to figure out which one was the first to be actually used. Other students may have their curiosity piqued and wonder the reasons for having two different stamps. Whenever posing a multistep search problem, be sure to also present this question: *Based on what you have discovered, what new questions can you ask?*

This may lead to a seemingly never-ending rabbit hole of questions and new searches for the answers. For example, a 5-cent stamp would allow you to mail a half-ounce letter 300 miles or less, and it cost 10 cents per half ounce for more than 300 miles. At this point, there are a great number of math problems that could be constructed with this information.

Students might also wonder, "How was mail sent before stamps were issued?" Others might be curious as to how much those stamps would be worth today. There is also the question of how much 5 and 10 cents would equate to in today's money. Considering the cost of a stamp today, how and when the cost has changed over time might be another question. Students might be interested to learn the cost of a stamp was 10 cents or less until 1975. Also, the cost of a stamp has actually decreased several times throughout history. When presented with new facts and information, students may wish to further investigate the topic. You should allow and encourage students to follow their curiosity down these new paths.

To help students develop the skill of locating information, I have created a series of multistep search problems for you and your students to explore. Note that although these are intended to require multiple steps in the search process, savvy Internet users may be able to construct a set of search terms that returns the answer with only one search. To assist you, I have included what I consider to be acceptable answers for each of the questions. The questions and answers can be found in Activity 3 in the handouts section of this chapter on pages 37–45—note that each question is on one side and the answers are on the other. See if you can't stump yourself a little too!

From Consumer to Producer

Now that you and your students have had some practice with finding answers to multistep search problems, the time has come to transition from consumer to producer. Although it can be challenging to find the answers to these questions, there is a different level of thinking that is required in creating a good multistep search problem. Encourage your students to develop questions based on their own interests, as they will have a deeper level of prior knowledge and can better craft challenging questions.

You might also have students use reference sources like an almanac or even *Guinness World Records* to find source material for their multistep search problems. Wikipedia can also be a great resource for finding ideas for questions. If you students are looking for ideas of where to begin you might point them to the following articles:

- List of highest-grossing films: https://en.wikipedia.org/wiki/List_of_highest-grossing_films
- List of world records in athletics: https://en.wikipedia.org/wiki/List_of_world_records_in_athletics
- List of Olympic records in athletics: https://en.wikipedia.org/wiki/List_of_Olympic_records_in_athletics
- List of roller coaster rankings: https://en.wikipedia.org/wiki/List_of_roller_coaster_rankings

As you and your students are creating your own multistep search problems, remember to attempt to construct problems that cannot be solved with a single search. Look for ways to create a set of questions. Finally, always remember to follow up by asking the question: *Based on what you have discovered, what new questions can you ask?*

Now that we have sharpened your students' skills related to locating information, we next set our sights on critically evaluating information that they encounter.

CHAPTER 4:
ACTIVITIES AND HANDOUTS

ACTIVITY 1

ONE CLICK

Directions: Examine the Google search results displayed below, and then answer the questions that follow.

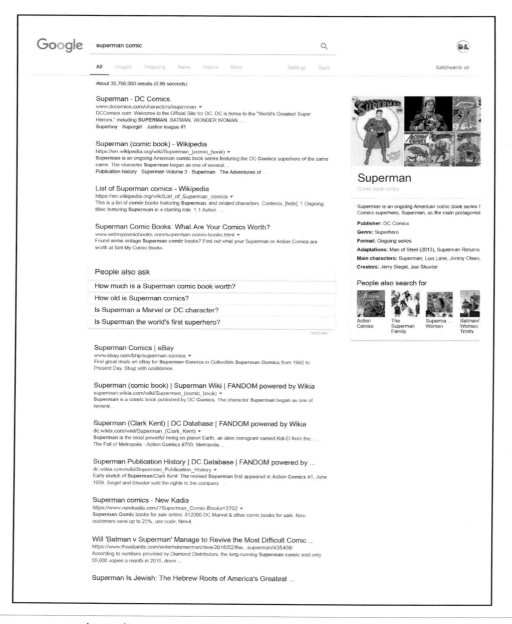

Superman search results page 1.

ACTIVITY 1, CONTINUED.

Superman search results page 1, *continued.*
Google and the Google logo are registered trademarks of Google Inc., used with permission.

Where on the page would you click to find answers to the following questions?

1. Who created Superman?

2. When and where did Superman first appear?

3. How much is a certain issue of a Superman comic worth?

ACTIVITY 1, CONTINUED.

4. Where could you buy past issues of a Superman comic?

5. Where can you find current information about Superman comics?

6. Where would you find information about Superman's alter ego?

7. What is Superman's real name? Hint: It is not the same as his alter ego.

8. Where could you find information about Lois Lane?

MARS SEARCH RESULTS

Directions: Practice the One Click strategy by looking at the Mars search results below and writing 5–8 questions you could ask a classmate related to the results.

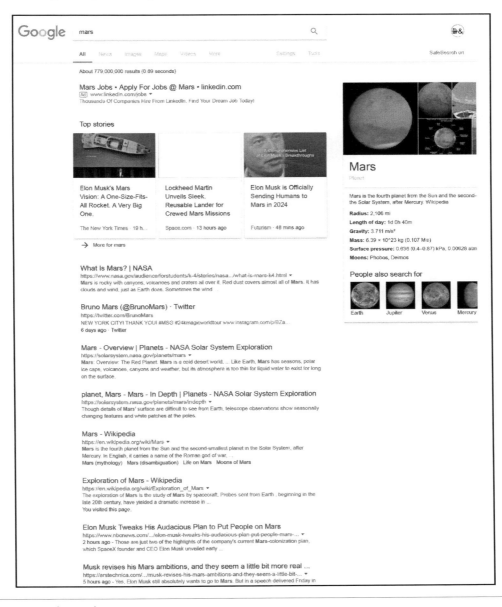

Mars search results page 1.

Google and the Google logo are registered trademarks of Google Inc., used with permission.

ACTIVITY 2, CONTINUED.

Adelaide, Australia, the founder of SpaceX opened the ...

People also ask

What is special about Mars?

What is on Mars the planet?

Why is it so important to go to Mars?

What does it look like on Mars?

NASA's Journey to Mars | NASA
https://www.nasa.gov/content/nasas-journey-to-mars
Mars is a rich destination for scientific discovery and robotic and human exploration as we expand our presence into the solar system. Its formation and evolution ...

The Planet Mars - Universe Today
https://www.universetoday.com/14701/mars/
Mars, otherwise known as the "Red Planet", is the fourth planet of our Solar System and the second smallest (after Mercury). Named after the ...

What Is Mars? | NASA
https://www.nasa.gov/audience/forstudents/5-8/features/nasa.../what-is-mars-58.html
Mars is the fourth planet from the sun and the next planet beyond Earth. It is, on average, more than 142 million miles from the sun. Mars is about one-sixth the ...

Searches related to mars

mars **information**	mars **surface**
mars **nasa**	mars **facts for kids**
mars **facts**	mars **distance from the sun**
mars **size**	**jupiter planet**

1 2 3 4 5 6 7 8 9 10   Next

Wilmington, North Carolina - From your internet address - Use precise location - Learn more

Help   Send feedback   Privacy   Terms

Mars search results page 1, *continued.*
Google and the Google logo are registered trademarks of Google Inc., used with permission.

Write your questions here:

_____

_____

_____

_____

_____

_____

_____

_____

MULTISTEP SEARCH PROBLEMS

Directions: To help develop your skills of locating information, explore the following multistep search problems. Although these problems are intended to require multiple steps in the search process, savvy Internet users may be able to construct a set of search terms that returns the answer with only one search. Are you up to the challenge?

Superhero Quotations

QUESTION: Often associated with a superhero, where did the quote "With great power there must also come—great responsibility" first appear? Who is the author of the quote?

Superman's Origins

QUESTION: Although you probably already know that Superman is from the planet Krypton, what is the Earth address of where Superman was created?

ACTIVITY 3, CONTINUED.

Superhero Quotations

ANSWER: This quote first appeared in the comic book *Amazing Fantasy #15* published in August of 1962. This comic features the first appearance of Spider-Man. In later Spider-Man films this quote is often presented as words of wisdom from Peter Parker's Uncle Ben. However, the quote appears in the final panel of the comic as a narrative description. Numerous others have been quoted throughout history using a very similar concept. For more information on the long history of this quote, refer to the blog entry from Quote Investigator at https://quoteinvestigator.com/2015/07/23/great-power.

Superman's Origins

ANSWER: Superman was created by an 18-year-old named Jerry Siegel in 1932. Jerry lived at 10622 Kimberly Avenue in Cleveland, OH. Joe Shuster, a high school classmate, first drew the character of Superman and lived less than a mile away on Amor Avenue.

Name: _____ Date: _____

Most Valuable Comic Book

QUESTION: What is the most ever paid for a comic book? When was it sold? How much did it originally sell for? What was the comic, and what makes this comic so special?

World's Fastest Animals

QUESTION: What are the fastest animals on land, in the air, and underwater?

ACTIVITY 3, CONTINUED.

Most Valuable Comic Book

ANSWER: The most ever paid for a comic book was $3.2 million. It was sold at auction in 2014. The comic was *Action Comics #1*. This comic is so special because it marks the first ever appearance of Superman. FYI: The second highest price ever paid from a comic was $1.1 million for a copy of *Amazing Fantasy #15*, which introduced Spider-Man.

World's Fastest Animals

ANSWER: When posing the question, "What is the fastest animal?" we are usually presented with the almost immediate response of cheetah, and although the cheetah can run at speeds of 70 miles per hour, it is hardly the fastest animal. This question will produce a wide variety of answers depending on a variety of conditions. Let's just say that there is a lot of debate about this topic. Most sources will point to the peregrine falcon being the fastest animal of all, with the capability of diving at speeds of more than 200 miles per hour. However, the spine-tailed swift has top flying speed of 106 mph without the aid of diving or wind currents. As we have already mentioned, the cheetah can reach a top speed of 70 mph, but it can only sustain this for a limited amount of time, while the pronghorn antelope can outsprint its predators at 60 mph. Finally, in the water, the title for the fastest fish belongs to the sail fish, which is capable of speeding through the water at 68 mph. To best answer this question, use multiple sources of information, as there seems to be a fair amount of discrepancy among various sources.

Video Games

QUESTION: What was the first commercially available video arcade game? When was it launched? What previous game was it based on, and what 1979 game did it later inspire?

Space Stuff

QUESTION: This dwarf planet is the largest object that lies between the orbits of Mars and Jupiter. What is its name? Who discovered it? When was it discovered? What was it the first of to be discovered?

ACTIVITY 3, CONTINUED.

Video Games

ANSWER: Although *Pong*, released in 1972, is often thought of to be the first arcade game, it was instead the first commercially *successful* game. Instead *Computer Space*, created by Syzygy was released in 1971. It was based on *Spacewar!* developed in 1962 by Steve Russell. However, *Spacewar!* was only playable on the DEC PDP-1, and only a handful of these computers existed in the world. *Computer Space* is remarkably similar to the 1979 game *Asteroids* that went on to achieve commercial success during the heyday of video arcades in the 1980s. For more information, check out this article from Wonderopolis: https://wonderopolis.org/wonder/who-invented-the-first-video-game.

Space Stuff

ANSWER: Students will probably first discover that between Mars and Jupiter lies an asteroid belt. Ceres was discovered by Giuseppe Piazzi on January 1, 1801, and it was the first asteroid ever to be discovered. Given its size and regular orbit, many now classify Ceres as a dwarf planet. For more information, check out the TED-Ed lesson at https://ed.ted.com/lessons/the-first-asteroid-ever-discovered-carrie-nugent.

ACTIVITY 3, CONTINUED.

A Viking and a Swift Astronomer

QUESTION: A Viking was the first to photograph us, but our existence was foretold in literature by a Swift astronomer. Who are we?

Money Saving Advice

QUESTION: In 2014, a 14-year-old middle school student suggested the U.S. government could save an estimated $234 million by doing what?

ACTIVITY 3, CONTINUED.

A Viking and a Swift Astronomer

ANSWER: The two moons of Mars, Phobos and Deimos. In *Gulliver's Travels,* Jonathan Swift references two moons of Mars. These moons had yet to be discovered at the time of the writing. In 1976, the Viking I spacecraft photographed the two moons of Mars.

Money Saving Advice

ANSWER: Suvir Mirchandani conducted a science fair project and concluded that the U.S. government could save $234 million by switching from using Times New Roman to the Garamond font for the printing of official documents. Garamond has thinner strokes and also allows for more characters to be printed in the same amount of space. For more information, check out this interview from CNN: http://www.cnn.com/2014/03/27/living/student-money-saving-typeface-garamond-schools/index.html.

ACTIVITY 3, CONTINUED.

Sports

QUESTION: This athlete is associated with the number 10. The theme song to a television soap opera was renamed after the athlete. Who was the athlete, what was the sport, and what is the significance of the number 10?

ACTIVITY 3, CONTINUED.

Sports

ANSWER: At the 1976 Summer Olympics in Montreal, Nadia Comaneci became the first gymnast to be awarded a perfect score of 10.0. During the games, she earned a total of seven 10s and won three gold medals. Originally named "Cotton's Dream," the theme song from *The Young and the Restless* was renamed "Nadia's Theme" after it was used in slow-motion montages of the gymnast on *ABC's Wide World of Sports*.

CRITICALLY EVALUATING INFORMATION

Once students have located the information that they are searching for, or in some cases, when the information has found its way to them, they must next take steps to critically evaluate the information. As we all learned from the original incarnation of Bloom's taxonomy, evaluation is the highest of the thinking skills. Critically evaluating information in digital environments can be a complicated process comprised of multiple steps and ways of viewing and thinking about the information. Having almost constant and instant access to vast amounts of information has conditioned us to far too often accept the information that is presented as fact without question. Instead, we should retrain ourselves and our students to resist the temptation to believe everything we see. We must adopt a healthy dose of skepticism and learn to question everything.

In this chapter, we will explore multiple methods for helping students to learn to critically evaluate information. This chapter represents the heart of the book and is perhaps the most important step in equipping students to fight fake news. To lay a firm foundation for your students' understanding, begin by having them determine the definitions of the following words and phrases. The next activity is designed to help you with this.

Begin by having your students locate definitions for the terms *information* and *evaluate* using a variety of dictionary sources. Emphasize that information is something that is factual and related to knowledge or intelligence. Next discuss that evaluation involves actively making a judgment about the value of something. Once the terms have been defined separately, have students consider what it means to *evaluate information*.

With this in mind, have students define *critically*. Many definitions highlight a level of disapproval. Be sure to emphasize that being critical is not necessarily a negative thing, but instead it involves a deep analysis of both the faults and merits of what is being examined. Now that all of three of the terms have been discussed, have students consider what it means to *critically evaluate information* and how that might differ from merely evaluating information, using Activity 4 on page 60.

Now that your students have developed an understanding of what it means to *critically evaluate information*, they are well on their way to becoming information skeptics. This is something that great philosophers and scientists have done throughout the ages. By helping students to learn to be more conscientious consumers of information, we are preparing them to be the next great thinkers.

THE CRAAP TEST

Developed by the Meriam Library at California State University, Chico, the CRAAP Test (http://library.csuchico.edu/help/source-or-information-good) offers a rather straightforward way to determine if the information that you find online is reliable information or not. Divided into five different strategies, the CRAAP Test provides a series of questions to help determine the quality and usefulness of the information (see CRAAP Test handout on p. 61).

Depending on the reading level of your students, the quantity and quality of the questions may be too advanced for them. Also, if you are working with elementary or even middle level students, you may not necessarily feel comfortable emphasizing the potential for stepping into "crap" online. That being said, the CRAAP Test does offer some important questions to consider for critically evaluating information.

THE CARS CHECKLIST

Another similar evaluation framework, developed by Robert Harris, is the CARS Checklist. CARS stands for Credibility, Accuracy, Reasonableness, and Support. Although there is a good deal of overlap between CARS and CRAAP, the CARS Checklist does not provide the same level of clarity and refinement in many of the questions that it poses. Like the CRAAP Test, it was originally created for college-level students to evaluate information while conducting Internet research. The handout on page 62 provides a summary of the CARS Checklist; for more detailed information on each of the four factors visit http://www.virtualsalt.com/evalu8it.htm.

CAPES: A GUIDE FOR EMPOWERING STUDENTS TO CRITICALLY EVALUATE INFORMATION

Taking inspiration from the CRAAP Test and the CARS Checklist, I looked for commonalities across the frameworks and also identified any important concepts that were not explicitly addressed. I then focused on what I considered to be the five most important factors for students to consider. What emerged was a new framework for students to utilize: CAPES: A Guide for Empowering Students to Critically Evaluate Information.

In Table 1, you can see how the three frameworks overlap with one another. The importance of accuracy of information is present in all three, although purpose and support are each present in only two of the frameworks. Although the CRAAP Test focuses on the authority of the source and the CARS Checklist describes this as credibility, CAPES combines those factors into the credentials of the source. A new factor for students to consider is emotion, or how the source of information makes them feel. Helping students to pay attention to how they might be responding on an emotional level rather that just an intellectual one is an important step in any critical examination of information.

What follows are introductory lessons for each of the five factors of the CAPES framework as well as a final challenge activity that combines all of the skills together in a search for truth.

Credentials

The first step in critically examining information is to determine who or what is the source of the information. Before deciding whether or not to believe a story, one should determine the credentials of the author and what qualifies him or her to report or share the information. By identifying the author, his or her level of expertise, and his or her bias, students will have a clearer understanding of the authenticity and reliability of the information being presented.

Begin by reviewing the definition of credentials provided in Activity 5 on page 63 with your students to determine their level of understanding of the concept. Next, provide them with a link to a news article on a topic of interest or one that you might currently be studying. Have the students locate the author of the information. On a surface level, they would identify the website where the information is located, but you really want have them dig deeper to find the author of that particular page or news story. Often there is a byline identifying the author of a news story if it is part of a larger media outlet. Students should look for information about the author or source of information. Sources often provide an About, About Me, Who We Are, or Biography page. The credentials might also be listed on the Contact page or even a Frequently Asked Questions (FAQ) page. By exploring what

Table 1

Comparison of the Three Methods

CAPES	CRAAP	CARS
	Currency	
	Relevancy	
Credentials	Authority	Credibility
Accuracy	Accuracy	Accuracy
Purpose	Purpose	
Emotion		
		Reasonableness
Support		Support

Note. Adapted from Meriam Library (n.d.) and Harris (2016).

the author is and even is not reporting about him- or herself, students can begin to gain some insight into the author's perspective, bias, and level of expertise.

However, when we only dig deeper for information about the author on the same site, what more do we hope to find? If the author is strongly biased either for or against the topic that he or she is reporting, he or she may intentionally hide this information on his or her own website. Instead, we want our students to think more like fact checkers. To do this, they must move quickly beyond close reading of the original text, and instead, they must learn to read laterally. Keeping the original source open, ask students to open up a series of tabs in their browser and search for information about the author or source of the information. Rather than just looking for more sources that report the same information, what do outside sources have to say about the bias and level of knowledge of the original source?

After digging deeper and reading laterally, ask the students to decide, based on the evidence that they have collected, how open or closed the author's bias is. What we have to realize is that there is almost always some bias present. Have students consider whether or not the author openly states his or her bias on the subject or if the bias is a closely guarded secret. Although it is ideal for the news media to be completely impartial, this is next to impossible. Instead, have students look for authors to clearly state their viewpoints in an open, rather than a closed, manner. Being open about one's bias may make that person a more trustworthy reporter on a given topic. However, bias is only one dimension to consider.

When locating information about the author or website, you and your students might gather information from the Internet Corporation for Assigned Names and Numbers or ICANN. This organization is responsible for assigning and cataloging all of the addresses and locations on the Internet. It provides a very useful Who Is? service (https://whois.icann.org) that will allow you to search for the owner of any website.

Savvy information consumers must also examine the level of knowledge or expertise of the author on the subject that is being reported. What is the background of the author? Does he or she have an advanced degree or training on the subject? Is the author a reporter with no experience on what is being reported? Has he or she reported on the subject before? As part of this level of examination, emphasize to your students the difference between something coming from an organization versus something that is said by a person. For example, news being reported by the United States Environmental Protection Agency should be viewed differently than a story being told by someone who happens to work for the Environmental Protection Agency. To further complicate matters, the current information from the EPA website may differ from the EPA Web Archive or the January 19, 2017, Web Snapshot available at https://19january2017snapshot.epa.gov, which preserves information regarding global warming and climate change that has been removed from the EPA website during the Trump administration.

After students have considered the author's bias and knowledge levels independently, have them examine the relationship between the two factors by plotting them on the provided matrix on page 64. Students should realize that sources that possess a novice level of knowledge and are closed about their bias are the least trustworthy. We want to gather information from sources that are considered to have expert levels of knowledge and are also open about their biases and perspectives on the subject. That being said, this matrix is not designed to be a foolproof measure of whether a source is reliable or not. Instead, it is meant to help students visualize how these two independent but related factors influence each other.

In *Star Wars: Episode IV—A New Hope* (Kurtz & Lucas,1977), a group of Stormtroopers stop Luke Skywalker, Obi-Wan Kenobi, R2-D2, and C-3PO on their way to the Mos Eisley spaceport. The Stormtroopers ask to see Luke's identification, but Obi-Wan quickly deflects them with what has become known as a Jedi mind trick. With the wave of his hand and the words, "You don't need to see his identification," our heroes are allowed to proceed without any Imperial entanglements. Do not let you students be fooled by Jedi mind tricks when consuming information. Rather, help them realize that they always need to check the identification and credentials of the sources of information before placing their trust in their authenticity.

Accuracy

After evaluating the credentials of the source, the next step in the CAPES framework is to determine the accuracy of the information that is being presented. The goal is to ensure that the information is factual, up to date, supported by evidence, and comprehensive. Accuracy is the one factor that exists in CAPES, the CRAAP Test, and the CARS Checklist. We want to be sure that the information that we are consuming and sharing is actually correct.

For Activity 6 on page 65, begin by reviewing the definition of accuracy provided. Lead students in conversation about the importance of having accurate information. Ask them if there seems to be anything missing from the definition. This will allow them to create a more personal connection and understanding of the term. Next, discuss the difference between facts and opinions. Point out that although something may be based on facts, it also may be influenced by the author's opinions or bias on the subject, and rather than thinking of information as being either fact or opinion, consider that it is on a continuum.

After this initial discussion, provide your students with a news story on a topic of interest or something currently being studied. Invite students to try out the second super searcher skill to determine the accuracy of the information. Begin by identifying where the information might fall on the opinion versus fact scale. They might do this as an initial response based on their gut reaction and then revisit it after going through the other sections.

Timeliness is a critical factor that can significantly influence the quality and usability of information. This is especially true when examining news stories. What may be timely information today may not be useful information tomorrow. This is also true of stories related to technology and innovation. Students need to realize that information is dynamic and constantly changing. When critically evaluating information, we should identify when the information was published and decide whether or not the information is up to date. Caution your students that many websites will automatically show today's date regardless of when the information was posted. If today's date is posted, proceed with caution and verify that indeed the information is from today.

The next step in identifying the accuracy of the information is to look for the supporting evidence for any claim that is being made. Is this information based on data and facts? Where does this evidence come from? Are the original sources of information cited? Any substantial claim that is being made should be supported by another source. We will dig deeper into this later when we get to the S in the CAPES, but at this point, students should start thinking about where the information is coming from.

Not only do we need to critically evaluate the information that is being provided on the site we are examining, we also should consider what information might be missing. In the next section of the Accuracy activity, have students "mind the gap" and think about any key details that are not being reported. As they are doing this, ask the question, "Does the story make sweeping generalizations or leap to unsupported conclusions?" These types of generalizations are often the stuff of fake news. Identifying the missing information can be almost as important as evaluating the information that is presented.

In the final step of the Accuracy activity, have students locate any errors in grammar and spelling. If the source contains multiple typographical errors or formatting issues, then that may be an indication of the level of professionalism and quality of the source. This is a good reminder to students that how they present their own work really does matter.

Purpose

As teachers in traditional reading environments, we have always sought to help our students understand and identify the author's purpose. I can remember vividly working with my fourth graders on this skill and using the acronym PIE: persuade, inform, and entertain. Information on the Internet or in digital environments is not necessarily that different in this regard, with the exception being that there are a great many sources that are trying to sell you something. The third super searcher strategy of CAPES focuses on the purpose of the information. To guide this section, we will use the acronym PIES.

Begin Activity 7 (see p. 67) by reviewing the definition of *purpose*. Next, have students create their own definitions for each of the four factors of PIES: persuade, inform, entertain, and sell. Discuss with them the difference between each of these four purposes. Have them locate an example of each purpose to demonstrate their understanding.

Next, provide them with a source of information to critically evaluate. Be sure to use an example that is on a topic of interest to the students in order to engage them in the learning process. Have the students identify the primary purpose of the information using the checklist provided in Activity 7. Depending on the source that you choose to share, there might be some overlap between more than one category. Have the students explain their rationale for determining the category.

Two scales have been provided for the students to rate the source of information. The first is to consider how clear or unclear the author's purpose is. Students should pay close attention to how the author is framing the information being shared. For example, students should be cautious when using a source that appears to have the purpose of informing, but the source is actually intended to persuade opinions. The second scale asks the students to identify whether the source is more objective (based in facts) or subjective (rooted in feelings). Again, there is often a continuum on this scale. With each scale, have students indicate why they rated the source the way that they did by providing evidence.

By examining it through the lens of purpose, students can gain a deeper understanding of why the information exists. Identifying whether something is intended to persuade, inform, entertain, or sell provides students with an important guide for how to best interpret and use the information.

Emotion

Perhaps the biggest lesson to learn when interacting with information and with others is how to monitor our own emotions. We are thinking and feeling beings, and we should recognize and acknowledge that much of the information that we are confronted with in digital environments is not only intended to reach us on an intellectual level, but, more likely than not, is also created with our emotions in mind. This emotional connection can be either a positive or negative experience. Many sources of information that are designed to persuade our thinking may cause us to feel outraged by their claims. Others may seek to gain our empathy and support in their cause.

To help your students better understand the role that their emotions play in critically evaluating information, introduce them to Robert Plutchik's theory of emotion, which identifies eight basic emotions: fear, anger, sadness, joy, disgust, surprise, trust, and anticipation. You and your students might recognize that five of the eight are characters from the Disney/Pixar film *Inside Out*. Plutchik (1980) expanded these basic eight emotions into what he referred to as the wheel of emotion where, based on the level of intensity, new emotions may emerge. However, working with only the eight basic emotions will serve our purposes here.

Begin by having students construct their own definitions of each of the eight emotions and identifying under which circumstances they might experience each. Plutchik (1980) proposed that the eight primary emotions were bipolar in nature: joy versus sadness, anger versus fear, trust versus disgust, and surprise versus anticipation. As part of the discussion of definitions, be sure to emphasize these relationships.

Next, provide students with a source of information. For this particular activity, a YouTube video might prove to be quite effective, as moving images and music may serve to incite their emotions. Try to select something that will appeal to your students' senses and is clearly designed to invoke some type of emotional response. After viewing the source, have your students identify which of the eight emotions that they felt, using the Activity 8 handout on page 69. Note that they may indicate feeling more than one emotion or a mixture of emotions. However, they probably will not have polar opposite responses to the prompt. For example, they are not very likely to experience joy and sadness simultaneously.

Then, have your students discuss the reasons why they feel these emotions and identify what specifically may have caused them to feel these emotions. Finally, it is critical to have students identify how their emotions are influencing their thinking. As part of the debriefing discussion, have students consider how having their thinking clouded by emotion may not lead to the most rational decision making. Although it is difficult to separate thoughts from emotions, having a level of awareness of the impact that our emotions have on our actions is a critical step in fighting fake news and critically evaluating information. By checking our emotions before we Tweet, repost, reply, or respond, we can proceed with clarity in our thinking.

Support

We have now reached the fifth and final factor of the CAPES framework: Support. Although each of the previous factors is incredibly important and necessary for critically evaluating information, the search for the truth may rest on whether or not any claim that a source is making can be supported by outside resources. Certainly, we have all heard the philosophical question, "If a tree falls in the forest and no one is around to hear it, does it make a sound?" Perhaps in the age of the Internet and fake news, an update to this question might be, "If only one person says something on the Internet or in the media, does it make it true?"

To combat fake news and to fight for the truth, we need to help our students to think more like fact checkers and be less like passive consumers of information. To do this, we have to teach them to read beyond the information that is on a single site or from a single source. As we have already seen in the credentials activity, we want our students to not only dig deeper into the source, but we want them to read laterally. In the credentials activity, they were looking to see who was saying the information. In Activity 9 (p. 71), Support, they are now looking for other sources to provide the same or similar information.

As with the previous activities, begin by discussing the definition provided. Pay close attention to the concept of corroboration and emphasize the increase in value of something when multiple sources make the same claim. Have students identify alternate definitions or explanations of the concept of support.

Next, provide an informational prompt for students to investigate. It might be interesting to provide something that is potentially a hoax or fake news. Then have the students review the prompt and identify what claim is being made. From there, students should seek three outside resources that support the claim being made. For an additional challenge, they might also try to locate information that contradicts the claim being made. The students should document the URL of the site and cite specific evidence that supports the original claim.

When we triangulate a claim with three other sources, we can get a clearer indication of whether or not the information is true or not. As you and your students are investigating the claim, emphasize the importance of looking at the information from multiple perspectives. Remember, because anyone can post anything that he or she wants on the Internet, it may not be enough to only locate three additional resources in support of the claim. Be on the lookout for dissenting points of view and be sure to weigh the evidence.

PUTTING ON THEIR CAPES

After students have had time to practice with each of the five areas in the CAPES framework, they are ready for a new challenge. Have the students equip themselves with their CAPES and go in search of the truth about the Yeti. Activity 10 (p. 72) was created because of my childhood fascination with the television series *In Search Of. . . .* Hosted by Leonard Nimoy, each week the show investigated a mysterious phenomena. It was highly sensationalized and filled with a cornucopia of conspiracy theories. At the beginning of each episode, a disclaimer was presented (Landsberg, 1977–1982):

> This series presents information based in part on theory and conjecture. The producer's purpose is to suggest some possible explanations, but not necessarily the only ones, to the mysteries we will examine.

In retrospect, this seems like a good reminder for almost any information that we might encounter on the Internet, through social media, or even in real life. In this activity, students will go in search of information to determine whether the Yeti is real or not. The Yeti was chosen for this challenge because of the high likelihood of distracting information related to the popular brand of coolers. Some students might choose to eliminate this distraction by using the search terms *yeti -cooler* only to find other products bearing the Yeti name, including a brand of high-end mountain bikes and also a brand of recording microphones. Once past this initial hurdle of commercial products, the quest should lead students to a wide variety of myths, legends, and conspiracy theories. Your Yeti hunters should work to locate three different and unrelated sources of information. Have them apply the CAPES framework for each of their sources and rate the source on a scale of 1 being an unreliable source, to 5 being trustworthy. Finally, it is up to your students to present the verdict that they reached based on their search while providing evidence of their conclusion.

From Consumer to Producer

Now that your students have developed their super search strategies by using the CAPES framework and uncovered some of the truth related to the mysteries of the Yeti, we want to help them further personalize their understanding of the CAPES. With their experiences in mind, challenge your students to create an infographic or comic to teach others about how to use CAPES. Although this type of activity may be done with any design tool, I suggest that you consider trying at least one the following:

- **Canva (https://www.canva.com):** Canva is a powerful web-based design tool that offers a large number of templates, fonts, and images for creating professional looking graphics.
- **Google Drawings (https://docs.google.com/drawings):** Part of the Google Drive suite of apps, this is probably the most powerful and least utilized tool for creativity and collaboration. Chances are that your students are already familiar with the way that Google Drive functions, making this is a great choice.
- **Comic Life (http://comiclife.com):** Comic Life offers a suite of tools for creating graphics and comic books. There are a number of different products here to try out. Make use of the free trial and then decide if this is the tool for you before purchasing.
- **Pixton Comics (https://www.pixton.com):** Pixton features a catalog of different cartoon characters that can be easily manipulated. This has the look and feel of a comic book and offers a lot of opportunity for creative expression.

Regardless of which tool you choose, I encourage you and your students to share your creations with everyone by posting online to various social networks using the hashtags #FightingFakeNews and #CAPES. For more information and to see what others have created, be sure to visit my website at http://brianhousand.com/fakenews.

CHAPTER 5:
ACTIVITIES AND HANDOUTS

Name: _____ Date: _____

DEFINITIONS

Directions: Define the terms listed below and answer the questions related to each defintion.

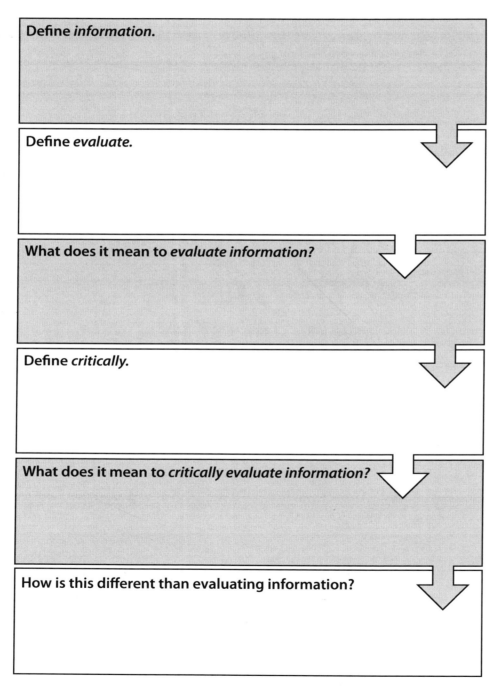

Define *information.*

Define *evaluate.*

What does it mean to *evaluate information?*

Define *critically.*

What does it mean to *critically evaluate information?*

How is this different than evaluating information?

Name: _____ Date: _____

THE CRAAP TEST

CURRENCY: THE TIMELINESS OF THE INFORMATION.
When was the information published or posted?
Has the information been revised or updated?
Does your topic require current information, or will older sources work as well?
Are the links functional?

RELEVANCE: THE IMPORTANCE OF THE INFORMATION FOR YOUR NEEDS.
Does the information relate to your topic or answer your question?
Who is the intended audience?
Is the information at an appropriate level (i.e. not too elementary or advanced for your needs)?
Have you looked at a variety of sources before determining this is the one you will use?
Would you be comfortable citing this source in your research paper?

AUTHORITY: THE SOURCE OF THE INFORMATION.
Who is the author / publisher / source / sponsor?
What are the author's credentials or organizational affiliations?
Is the author qualified to write on the topic?
Is there contact information, such as a publisher or email address?
Does the URL reveal anything about the author or source (examples: .com .edu .gov .org .net)?

ACCURACY: THE RELIABILITY, TRUTHFULNESS AND CORRECTNESS OF THE CONTENT.
Where does the information come from?
Is the information supported by evidence?
Has the information been reviewed or refereed?
Can you verify any of the information in another source or from personal knowledge?
Does the language or tone seem unbiased and free of emotion?
Are there spelling, grammar or typographical errors?

PURPOSE: THE REASON THE INFORMATION EXISTS.
What is the purpose of the information? Is it to inform, teach, sell, entertain or persuade?
Do the authors / sponsors make their intentions or purpose clear?
Is the information fact, opinion or propaganda?
Does the point of view appear objective and impartial?
Are there political, ideological, cultural, religious, institutional or personal biases?

THE CARS CHECKLIST FOR RESEARCH SOURCE EVALUATION

CREDIBILITY	**GOAL:** An authoritative source that supplies good evidence that allows you to trust it **SUMMARY:** Trustworthy source, author's credentials, evidence of quality control, known or respected authority, organizational support
ACCURACY	**GOAL:** A source that is correct today (not yesterday) and one that gives the whole truth **SUMMARY:** Up to date, factual, detailed, exact, comprehensive, audience and purpose reflect intentions of completeness and accuracy
REASONABLENESS	**GOAL:** A source that engages the subject thoughtfully and reasonably, concerned with the truth **SUMMARY:** Fair, balanced, objective, reasoned, no conflict of interest, absence of fallacies or slanted tone
SUPPORT	**GOAL:** A source that provides convincing evidence for the claims made, a source you can triangulate (find at least two other sources that support it) **SUMMARY:** Listed sources, contact information, available corroboration, claims supported, documentation supplied

Note. Adapted from Harris, 2016.

CREDENTIALS

Directions: Review the definition of credentials, then use the link provided by your teacher to answer each question below.

CREDENTIALS

Definition: A qualification, achievement, personal quality, or aspect of a person's background, typically when used to indicate that he or she is suitable for something.

Who or What Is the Source of the Information?

First: Dig deeper.
What did you learn from the About page?

Next: Read laterally.
What other information can you find about the author or source of information?

Decide: How open or closed is their bias? What makes you say that?

Then: What makes the source an expert on the subject?

ACTIVITY 5, CONTINUED.

Plot the Bias and Knowledge Level of the Author.

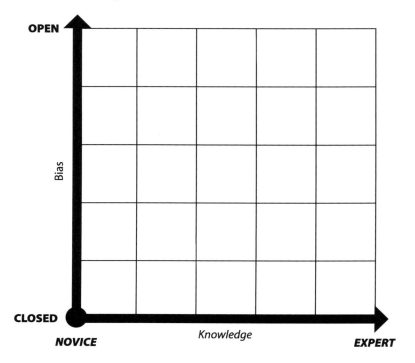

Finally: What conclusions can you make regarding the credentials of the author?

Name: _____ Date: _____

ACCURACY

Directions: Use the news story provided by your teacher to practice determining the accuracy of a source.

ACCURACY

Definition: The condition or quality of being true, correct, or exact; freedom from error or defect; precision or exactness; correctness.

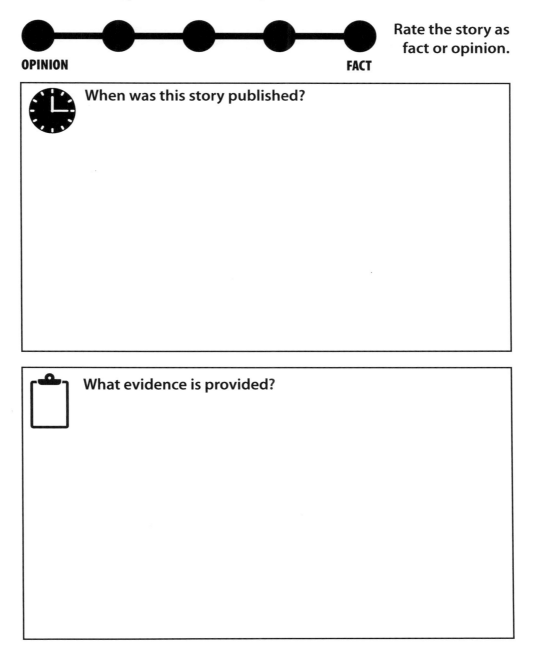

● ━ ● ━ ● ━ ● ━ ● **Rate the story as fact or opinion.**

OPINION   **FACT**

🕐 **When was this story published?**

📋 **What evidence is provided?**

ACTIVITY 6, CONTINUED.

 What important details are missing?

Is the information free from spelling and grammar errors? If not, what does this tell you about the quality of the source?

PURPOSE

Directions: First, define each type of purpose. Then mark the purpose of the link provided by your teacher and expain how you came to that decision.

PURPOSE

Definition: the reason for which something exists or is done, made, used, etc.

There are four primary purposes for information to exist.
Define each purpose next to the icon for that purpose.

PERSUADE

INFORM

ENTERTAIN

SELL

MARK THE PURPOSE: ☐ **PERSUADE** ☐ **ENTERTAIN** ☐ **INFORM** ☐ **SELL**

How did you determine the purpose?

ACTIVITY 7, CONTINUED.

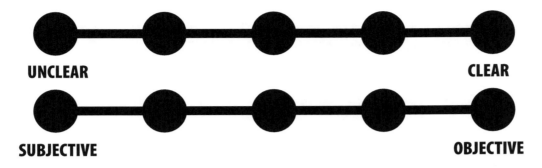

UNCLEAR **CLEAR**

SUBJECTIVE **OBJECTIVE**

Is the author's purpose clear or unclear?

What makes you say that?

Is the point of view subjective or objective?

What makes you say that?

Name: _____ Date: _____

EMOTION

Directions: View the source provided by your teacher and mark which emotions you feel. Were you surprised by any of these emotions? Explain on the following page how the source affected your emotions.

EMOTION

Definition: Instinctive or intuitive feeling as distinguished from reasoning or knowledge; any strong agitation of feelings usually accompanied by certain physiological changes.

Name: _____ Date: _____

After viewing the source, what emotions do you feel?

Why do you feel these emotions?

List any other emotions that you are feeling.

What causes you to feel these emotions?

How are your emotions influencing your thinking?

Name: _____ Date: _____

SUPPORT

Directions: Review the informational prompt provided by your teacher. Then, examine the claim made by the prompt and find additional sources to support it.

SUPPORT

Definition: To hold up or serve as a foundation or prop for; to uphold or defend as valid or right; suggest the truth of; corroborate.

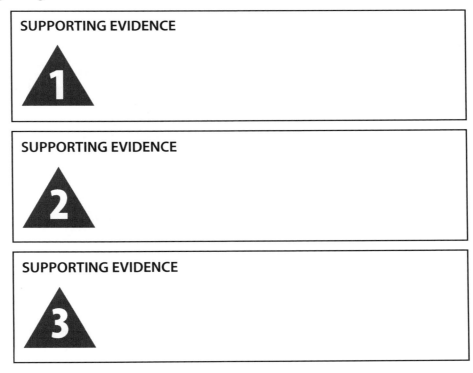

CLAIM: What claim is being made? Who is making this claim?

Triangulate the claim with three other sources. For each source, include the URL and supporting evidence from the website.

SUPPORTING EVIDENCE

1

SUPPORTING EVIDENCE

2

SUPPORTING EVIDENCE

3

ACTIVITY 10

YETI ACTIVITY

Directions: According to Wikipedia (n.d.), the Yeti is "an ape-like entity, taller than the average human, that is said to inhabit the Himalayan region of Nepal, Bhutan, and Tibet." Using your Internet Searching Superpowers and the CAPES guide, can you find three sources that prove whether or not the Yeti is real?

Name: _____ Date: _____

C	**SOURCE 1** *Name and URL*	
	CREDENTIALS *Who is the author?* *What makes the* *author an expert?* *What is his or her* *bias?*	
A	**ACCURACY** *Is the information up* *to date?* *Is the information* *based on facts?* *Where did the* *information come* *from?*	
P	**PURPOSE** *What is the purpose?* *Inform? Entertain?* *Satire? Parody?* *Advertisement?* *News?*	
E	**EMOTION** *Is the site designed to* *evoke an emotional* *response?* *How does this site* *make you feel?*	
S	**SUPPORT** *What supporting* *evidence can you find* *from another site?*	

RATE THIS SOURCE				
1 **UNRELIABLE**	2	3	4	5 **TRUSTWORTHY**

ACTIVITY 10, CONTINUED.

	SOURCE 2 *Name and URL*	
C	**CREDENTIALS** *Who is the author?* *What makes the* *author an expert?* *What is his or her* *bias?*	
A	**ACCURACY** *Is the information up* *to date?* *Is the information* *based on facts?* *Where did the* *information come* *from?*	
P	**PURPOSE** *What is the purpose?* *Inform? Entertain?* *Satire? Parody?* *Advertisement?* *News?*	
E	**EMOTION** *Is the site designed to* *evoke an emotional* *response?* *How does this site* *make you feel?*	
S	**SUPPORT** *What supporting* *evidence can you find* *from another site?*	

RATE THIS SOURCE				
1 **UNRELIABLE**	**2**	**3**	**4**	**5** **TRUSTWORTHY**

Name: _____ Date: _____

	SOURCE 3 *Name and URL*	
C	**CREDENTIALS** *Who is the author?* *What makes the author an expert?* *What is his or her bias?*	
A	**ACCURACY** *Is the information up to date?* *Is the information based on facts?* *Where did the information come from?*	
P	**PURPOSE** *What is the purpose?* *Inform? Entertain?* *Satire? Parody?* *Advertisement?* *News?*	
E	**EMOTION** *Is the site designed to evoke an emotional response?* *How does this site make you feel?*	
S	**SUPPORT** *What supporting evidence can you find from another site?*	

RATE THIS SOURCE				
1 **UNRELIABLE**	**2**	**3**	**4**	**5** **TRUSTWORTHY**

ACTIVITY 10, CONTINUED.

The Verdict

Based on your investigation, does the Yeti exist, or is the Yeti only a legend? Provide evidence and describe how you reached your verdict.

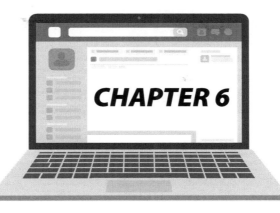

CHAPTER 6

SYNTHESIZING INFORMATION

Now that we have developed your students' ability to critically evaluate information, we next need to hone their skills related to synthesizing information. When interacting with information, we are seldom dealing with only one source. Instead, we are often overwhelmed by multiple sources of information. We must also be able to determine where that information fits into our existing schema, prior knowledge, and current understanding. This is no small feat.

SUMMARY VERSUS SYNTHESIS

While teaching reading, we have long sought to help our students understand how to summarize information. As an elementary teacher and even as a university professor, I have often seen my students struggle with their ability to effectively summarize information. Let us first consider what a summary is.

Summary = Covering the Main Points Succinctly

Identifying the most essential information from a source of information can prove challenging for our students. Students seem to either include too much information or too little information in their summaries. When we are summarizing, we are typically only dealing with one source of information. For example, we might ask students to read a chapter or a passage of text and provide a summary of the events or information. However, outside of a reading class things tend to be much more complicated.

Instead, much of what our students must do when interacting with information, especially in digital environments, is to synthesize a variety of sources to form an understanding. Consider the definition of *synthesis* in the next section and how it compares to that of *summary*.

Synthesis = The Combining of Often Diverse Conceptions Into a Coherent Whole

Thanks to the original Bloom's taxonomy (Bloom et al., 1956), synthesis has long been held up as the epitome of higher order thinking, and rightfully so. The ability to successfully combine a wide range of ideas into a new, personal understanding is quite remarkable and at times something of a mystery. Unlike many of the other levels of Bloom's taxonomy, synthesis is typically more difficult to observe, as it primarily takes place in the brain and is not necessarily demonstrated by an action. Perhaps this is the reason that synthesis was removed from the revised Bloom's taxonomy.

When the taxonomy was revised in 2001, nouns were changed to verbs to reflect that thinking should be active (see Figure 9). The top two levels of the 1956 Taxonomy (Synthesis and Evaluation) were switched, and synthesis was transformed into Create. When I first saw this, I was delighted that creating was being emphasized for our students. However, part of me really missed synthesis. As we look at the world around us and the rise of fake news, synthesis may be more important now than ever before.

As I sought to develop a deeper understanding of this switch, I came across a 1996 interview in *Wired Magazine* with Steve Jobs, conducted by Gary Wolf. In this interview, Jobs eloquently described the creative process and its relationship to synthesizing;

> Creativity is just connecting things. When you ask creative people how they did something, they feel a little guilty because they didn't really do it, they just saw something. It seemed obvious to them after a while. That's because they were able to connect experiences they've had and synthesize new things. And the reason they were able to do that was that they've had more experiences or they have thought more about their experiences than other people. (para. 135)

The entire interview as it was published can be accessed at https://www.wired.com/1996/02/jobs-2.

In Steve Jobs's view, those who are most creative are those individuals that have had the most experiences or exposure to a wide range of topics. These topics are not necessarily part of the standardized curriculum. Instead, these experiences are

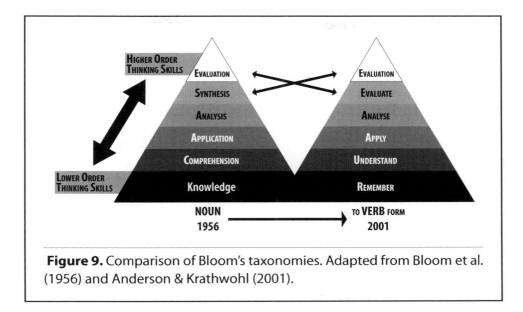

Figure 9. Comparison of Bloom's taxonomies. Adapted from Bloom et al. (1956) and Anderson & Krathwohl (2001).

often based in our own interests. Additionally, these interests are often unrelated to one another.

In *A Whole New Mind*, Daniel Pink (2005) described this in a similar manner. As we enter a Conceptual Age, those who hope to thrive will "know how to link apparently unconnected elements to create something new" (p. 110). This idea is especially important when it comes to fighting fake news. As we encounter new information and ideas, we must work to discern how this aligns or contradicts with our current understanding while finding connections between what is known and what is being learned.

To build your students' capacity for making connections, I suggest creating a set of experiences for your students that I am calling Wikipedia Golf. This whole idea stems from my own experiences in the mid 1990s when I got my first computer with a CD-ROM drive. As was customary back in the day, a new computer purchase also bought you a set CD-ROMs. Some were definitely more useful than others. The one that I was most excited about and spent the most time with was *Encarta*. Now, I had always loved the encyclopedia growing up and often found myself looking things up just for fun. *Encarta* brought this love of learning and discovering to a whole new level because it introduced something that we all now take for granted: hypertext.

The ability to be reading an article and to simply click on a hyperlink and be instantly transported to another article on a related topic was exactly the type of "rabbit hole" that my curious mind had always longed for. I cannot tell you the number of hours and even days that I spent perusing *Encarta* and filling my brain with a wide range of information that I did not even know that I was interested in learning.

BUILDING CONNECTIONS
WITH WIKIPEDIA GOLF

Wikipedia Golf takes this idea of "rabbit hole" exploration from my time with *Encarta* and transforms it into a game of exploration and connection building for your students. The idea is this: What is the least number of clicks that will take you from one entry on Wikipedia to a seemingly unrelated entry? The only way that you can move forward is by selecting a hyperlink on an existing page. For example, how many clicks would it take to go from Albus Dumbledore to Honey Bee?

Although at first glance, these two things might seem that completely unrelated, by reading the Wikipedia entry for Albus Dumbledore we learn that the name Dumbledore is an early modern English word for "bumblebee," and that because of his love of music, J. K. Rowling envisioned him humming to himself a lot.

Click one is obviously "bumblebee." We then learn that bumblebees are social insects and form colonies, however, these colonies are smaller than those of "honey bees." Click two and we have arrived at our goal! Certainly, not every round of Wikipedia Golf is going to be quite this easy, but with some practice you might find that, like Kevin Bacon, there are often only six degrees of separation between almost anyone and anything.

Tip: Use the Find Feature!

One critical strategy in Wikipedia Golf is to make use of the Find function in your web browser. You can select this from the Edit menu or by using Command + F on a Mac or CTRL + F on a PC. This will activate a search box that allows you to enter a word or phrase. All uses on the current webpage will be highlighted. This allows you to quickly see whether or not a word exists on the page. The Find function is incredibly helpful not only when playing Wikipedia Golf, but when searching for any piece of information.

Activity 11 (p. 86) is a collection of potential topics to use for your own game of Wikipedia Golf, along with a scoring sheet. I have assembled 20 different entries in seven categories for you and your students to choose from. I purposefully selected each entry based on topics that might be of interest to your students and the quality of the entry. More specifically, I selected pages that included a wide variety of links to other Wikipedia entries. You might first try selecting two entries from the same category and providing an example how best to go about navigating from Point A to Point B. An example of how to go from Amelia Earhart to Buzz Lightyear in five clicks has been provided for you in Handout 3 on page 95.

When looking for connections, it is often helpful to burn the candle at both ends or to search from both the beginning and ending points. Try opening up two separate tabs or windows with each of the searches and then working toward the middle. What may not be an obvious connection at first often becomes very apparent in a few clicks. Note that, like most things in life, this does become easier with practice and experience. That being said, not every combination may be possible. Have students challenge each other to find a solution and then challenge others to make the same connection in the same or fewer clicks.

Remember the goal here is to allow students to build their background knowledge while looking for connections between seemingly unrelated topics. Making these connections is one hallmark of synthesis and a creative mind.

From Consumer to Producer: Two Abraham Lincolns and a Pinocchio

Although there certainly is no shortage of Wikipedia Golf challenges that you and your students could assemble, I want to encourage you to help develop your students' ability to synthesize information even further. In Activity 12 (see p. 96), your students will work to locate three sources of information. Two of the sources are true, and one of the sources is inaccurate. This activity is based on the Bluff the Listener game from my favorite NPR radio program, *Wait, Wait . . . Don't Tell Me!* The premise of the game is that the three celebrity panelists each tell a story about a common theme, but only one of the stories is true. The caller then has to guess which one of the stories is true. If you are not familiar with the program, try searching for *Bluff the Listener*. You will find a multitude of examples to listen to. To introduce your students to the activity, consider playing one of the segments for them. You should preview the segment to determine that the content is appropriate for your students. Unlike in the *Bluff the Listener* game, your students should locate two Abraham Lincolns, or true stories, instead of only one. Based on my experiences in completing this activity working with students and teachers, it works much better to have only one false story. Page 96 includes the activity guide to share with your students to get them started.

After your students have compiled their stories, I encourage you to share them online via social media using the hashtags #FightingFakeNews and #2Lincolns1Pinocchio. Also, visit http://brianhousand.com/fakenews to see examples that I have gathered from others.

In order to better equip ourselves and our students in the fight against fake news, we have explored options for developing the skills of synthesizing information. Purveyors of fake news often rely on making false connections between seemingly related topics. Such is the stuff of conspiracy theories and conjecture. To help our students be more aware of fake news, we should help them understand the tricks of the trade. Indeed, this is not new advice, for in *The Art of War*, Sun Tzu wrote:

> Know the enemy and know yourself; in a hundred battles you
> will never be in peril.
> When you are ignorant of the enemy but know yourself, your
> chances of winning or losing are equal.
> If ignorant both of your enemy and of yourself, you are certain
> in every battle to be in peril. (p. 84)

The hope is that by experiencing multiple rounds of Wikipedia Golf that your students will develop a broader background knowledge and be able to more readily see connections and synthesize information. By examining these connections, and even seeking to share some fake news of their own through the Two Abraham Lincolns and a Pinocchio activity, they will develop a deeper understanding of themselves and the enemy of fake news.

CHAPTER 6:
ACTIVITIES AND HANDOUTS

ACTIVITY 11

WIKIPEDIA GOLF

Directions: Choose two items listed in the following charts. TEE UP by entering your starting point in the SEARCH BOX on Wikipedia.org. By only clicking on hyperlinks in Wikipedia, what is the least amount of clicks that you can use to reach the goal? Use the accompanying score card to record your "clicks" and to describe your thinking. *Hint*: Using the Find feature will help you locate key words on the page.

PEOPLE	Harrison Ford	Oprah Winfrey
Albert Einstein	J. K. Rowling	Queen Victoria
Amelia Earhart	LeBron James	Stan Lee
Anne Frank	Louis Armstrong	Steve Jobs
Charlie Chaplin	Malala Yousafzai	Taylor Swift
Eleanor Roosevelt	Marie Curie	Walt Disney
Elon Musk	Nadia Comăneci	William Shakespeare

ACTIVITY 11, CONTINUED.

CHARACTERS	Hermione Granger	Pippi Longstocking
Albus Dumbledore	Katniss Everdeen	Princess Leia
Batman	Kermit the Frog	R2-D2
Buzz Lightyear	Mary Poppins	Sherlock Holmes
Captain America	Minnie Mouse	The Cat in the Hat
Dorothy Gale	Peter Pan	Willy Wonka
Frodo Baggins	Pikachu	Wonder Woman

ANIMALS	hippopotamus	scorpion
banana slug	honey bee	sloth
echidna	jellyfish	spider monkey
flamingo	kangaroo	tiger
giant panda	peacock	tortoise
giant squid	salamander	Tyrannosaurus rex
grizzly bear	salmon	whale shark

ACTIVITY 11, CONTINUED.

PLACES	Golden Gate Bridge	Parthenon
baggage claim	Grand Canyon	Silicon Valley
Berlin Wall	Great Barrier Reef	Sphinx
Camelot	Great Wall of China	Stonehenge
Detroit	lemonade stand	The Oregon Trail
drive-in theater	Mars	Venice
Eiffel Tower	Mount Everest	voting booth

FOODS	croissant	pistachio
avocado	doughnut	pizza
bacon	fortune cookie	SPAM
breakfast cereal	hot dog	strawberry
buffalo wing	lasagna	sushi
candy	orange juice	tacos
cheese	pancake	tomato

ACTIVITY 11, CONTINUED.

EVENTS	Groundhog Day	September 11
birthday	Hurricane Katrina	sinking of the RMS Titanic
Brexit	Lewis and Clark expedition	snow
carnival	moon landing	solar eclipse
Election Day	Olympic Games	Super Bowl
Fourth of July	picnic	vacation
Gold Rush	press conference	World's Fair

Name: _____ Date: _____

THINGS	food truck	paper airplane
bar code	foosball	parking meter
Bigfoot	Helvetica	PEZ
Bitcoin	LEGO	solar panel
comic book	Minecraft	Swiss Army knife
crossword puzzle	Ford Model T	totem pole
Ferris wheel	Nintendo	unicorn

ACTIVITY 11, CONTINUED.

WIKIPEDIA GOLF

	ENTRY	THINKING
START		
CLICK 1		
CLICK 2		
CLICK 3		
CLICK 4		
CLICK 5		
CLICK 6		
CLICK 7		
CLICK 8		
CLICK 9		
CLICK 10		
GOAL		

WIKIPEDIA GOLF SAMPLE SCORECARD

WIKIPEDIA GOLF

	ENTRY	THINKING
START	Amelia Earhart	Enter your starting point in the box to the left. Use the boxes below to comment on your thinking in the process.
CLICK 1	aviation pioneer	Searched for SPACE and found link to National Air and Space Museum.
CLICK 2	National Air and Space Museum	
CLICK 3	Apollo 11	
CLICK 4	Buzz Aldrin	Buzz Aldrin inspired the name of the *Toy Story* character. Aldrin acknowledged the tribute when he pulled a Buzz Lightyear doll out during a speech at NASA.
CLICK 5	Buzz Lightyear	
CLICK 6		
CLICK 7		
CLICK 8		
CLICK 9		
CLICK 10		
GOAL	Buzz Lightyear	Enter your GOAL in the box to the left.

ACTIVITY 12

TWO ABRAHAM LINCOLNS AND A PINNOCCHIO

Directions:

1. Locate two news stories or websites that seem unlikely but are factual.

2. Find one news story or website that is at least somewhat plausible but is false.

3. Create a Google Doc or Slides presentation that contains the three stories.

4. Bonus points if the three stories are related or focused on one topic.

CHAPTER 7

COMMUNICATING INFORMATION

In our digital age, we are bombarded by an ever-growing number of media outlets and tools for communication. These tools offer the promise of constructing social networks and afford us the opportunity to connect with almost anyone at any time and in any place. With the passing of time, new outlets for communication are introduced on a regular basis. Keeping up with this ever-changing digital landscape is especially challenging given that even the tools that we have come to rely on are constantly being updated and tweaked for efficiency.

To further complicate matters, our students often seem to be two steps ahead of us when it comes to the adoption of social media tools. Often just when we get comfortable using a platform, our students are using a different tool altogether. Rather than attempting to address every tool that you and your students might utilize and running the risk of creating a book that is quickly out of date, I will instead focus on two tools that have stood the test of time (Facebook and Twitter) and offer some common sense strategies for fighting fake news in these and other environments like them.

FACEBOOK

I can remember very vividly conducting a training with a group of middle school gifted teachers in 2010 and hearing one teacher share a story of one of her brightest students and his use of Facebook. As part of a unit on propaganda, the students in the class were discussing where they got their news and information from. Most students indicated that they got news from news websites. However, there was one student who boldly claimed that he got all of his news from Facebook. The teacher recounted being shocked by this statement and decided to probe further by asking, "You do know that Facebook is not really 'news,' don't you?" The student responded, "Well, then why does it say 'News Feed' on the page?"

At the time, it seemed both funny and a little frightening, but as I reflect on the experience today, it is all too close to the truth. Although this does serve as a cautionary tale, it helps us to realize that although out students may be natives in a digital world, they may also lack a basic understanding of what is and is not news. In the student's defense, news is generally defined as newly received or noteworthy information. For many of our students, reading what their friends and family are up to might seem more newsworthy than the latest national news. Helping our students to understand the larger world is one of the ongoing challenges that we face as educators.

The Three Dots of Facebook

As a tool, Facebook is filled with features that you and your students are probably not utilizing to their fullest. Many of these features are hiding in plain sight right behind the three dots of Facebook.

• • •

You have probably seen these three dots or ellipsis before. They are part of every single post on Facebook, but have you ever clicked on them to see what secrets they hold? You should try it. Go on, click them. You know you want to. I'll wait.

Now that you are back, what did you find? Were you surprised by what was there? Did you find all of the features? Let's go through some of the possibilities together and discuss how you and your students might go about using your new powers.

There are three basic types of posts that you will encounter on Facebook.

1. **Friends' Posts:** This is original content that is usually text-based, but may also include an uploaded photo or video.
2. **Friends' Posts With a Shared Link:** This is a post from a friend that includes a link to an external website or content previously posted by someone else on Facebook.
3. **Sponsored or Suggested Posts:** This is paid content or an advertisement posted to Facebook based on your interests or Internet search history.

Friends' Posts

When a friend posts original content, then the three dots of Facebook presents the image in Figure 10.

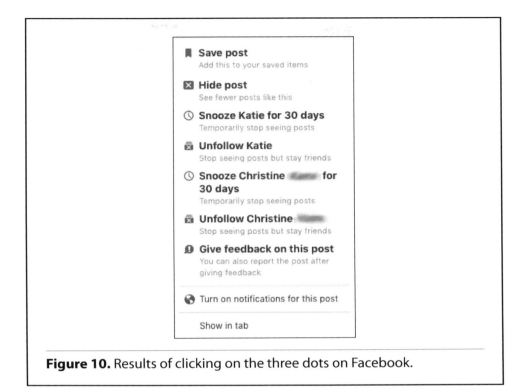

Figure 10. Results of clicking on the three dots on Facebook.

This is an original post from my Facebook friend, Katie, that has comments from a mutual friend Christine. In addition to the usual options of *Like*, *Comment*, and *Share*, clicking on the three dots opens a new menu.

Save post. We can now choose to save the post, which works like a bookmark within Facebook. You can view all of your saved posts by choosing *Saved* from the *Explore* menu on the left side of the screen or by going to https://www.facebook.com/saved. This is quite useful when you want to be able to quickly recall a particular post from your friend at a later date.

Hide post. If your friend posts something that you would rather not see, then you can choose to hide his or her posts. This will still keep you as friends, but posts from him or her will appear less frequently in your News Feed.

Snooze for 30 days. This will put a temporary hold on you seeing any posts from this friend. You will still remain Facebook friends and you can still see posts by going to his or her feed, but these posts will not appear in your News Feed.

Unfollow. This will put a permanent block on seeing posts from this person, but you will still remain Facebook friends. Of course, you always have to option to simply "unfriend" someone, but depending on your relationship, this may not be the best option.

When a mutual Facebook friend comments on a friend's post, you also have the option to *Snooze* or *Unfollow* that friend from this menu. This is useful if you have a mutual friend who frequently posts annoying or irrelevant comments.

Give feedback on this post. When confronted with a post that is inappropriate, the three dots of Facebook allow you to give feedback on the post and help

Facebook to monitor similar posts. In Figure 11, you can see the eight categories that Facebook is interested in controlling, with one of them being "false news." As good digital citizens, we have the moral obligation to report posts that are potentially harmful to others.

Friends' Posts With a Shared Link

Many times, you or your friends will come across interesting links on Facebook or the Internet that you want to share with others. For posts like this, Facebook offers a slightly different set of options. Although you can still *Hide* a post, *Snooze* posts from your friend, *Unfollow* your friend, and *Give feedback on this post*, you now have the ability to hide and snooze content from the source of the information (see Figure 12).

In Figure 12, you can see the options available to you when a friend shares content from TED. If you are simply getting too much information from a particular source or it does not meet you needs, then you have options to control how much content you are receiving. Having the ability to control the content that you are seeing is a powerful tool in fighting fake news.

Sponsored or Suggested Post

Whether we realize it or not, Facebook and most of the Internet services that we take for granted are made possible by the revenue that is generated from advertisements. Facebook explains how it uses advertising to create an personalized experience for you on the "About Facebook Ads" page available at https://www.facebook.com/ads/about.

Advertisements may appear as posts in your News Feed and are identified by the terms *sponsored* or *suggested*. Perhaps not surprisingly, these terms are written in a smaller font in a muted grey tone, which makes them a bit less conspicuous.

Clicking on the three dots reveals another new menu (see Figure 13).

From this menu, we can choose to save a link to the advertised content, as we did with the other saved links—it also will appear at https://www.facebook.com/saved. We can also choose to *Hide* an ad to see fewer ads like this one in our News Feed. This menu also offers some new options as well.

First, we have the ability to *Report ad* to mark an ad as offensive or inappropriate. Choosing this option opens up the menu in Figure 14.

Facebook wants us to help it understand what is happening and why you feel that the ad is inappropriate. One of the eight options available is "It's a false news story." Reporting advertisements that are inappropriate is part of our responsibility as digital citizens.

Facebook is also happy to share with you why sponsored content was added to your News Feed. By clicking on *Why am I seeing this?*, a new information box appears to reveal the target audience for the ad. From this screen you may choose to block all

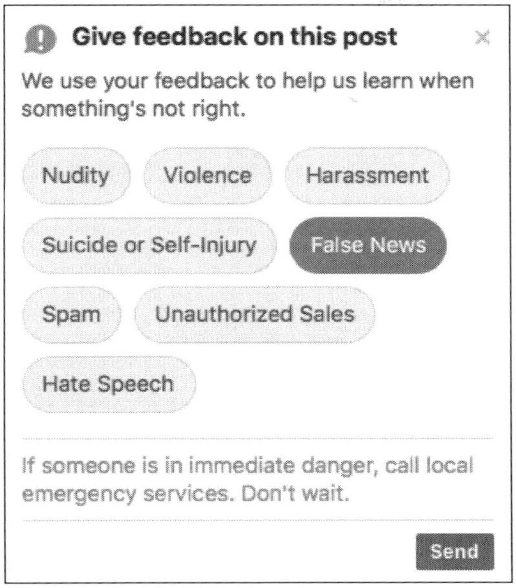

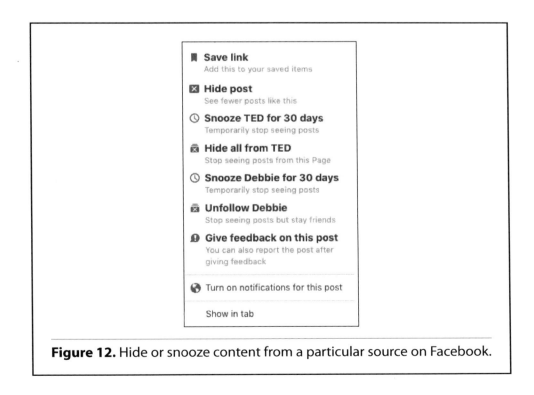

Figure 11. Option for providing feedback to Facebook.

Figure 12. Hide or snooze content from a particular source on Facebook.

Figure 13. The three dots related to ads on Facebook.

Figure 14. Options for reporting ads.

ads from this advertiser in the Options menu. Even more powerful is the ability to *Manage Your Ad Preferences*. You can access this directly by visiting https://www.facebook.com/ads/preferences. Here you are able to customize and even limit the information that you choose to share with Facebook.

One final option available in the menu is to report that the ad is useful. This is a surefire way to ensure that you will see more advertisements and sponsored content from this source.

From Consumer to Producer

Facebook recognizes that fake news (or as it refers to it, *false news*) is often spread using its platform. To combat this, Facebook has chosen to focus on three key areas (Mosseir, 2017):

- **disrupting economic incentives,** because most false news is financially motivated;
- **building new products** to curb the spread of false news; and
- **helping people make more informed decisions** when they encounter false news. (para. 2)

To help users better identify false news, Facebook (n.d.) put together 10 suggestions for spotting false news (see Handout 4, p. 111):

1. BE SKEPTICAL OF HEADLINES.
2. LOOK CLOSELY AT THE URL.
3. INVESTIGATE THE SOURCE.
4. WATCH FOR UNUSUAL FORMATTING.
5. CONSIDER THE PHOTOS.
6. INSPECT THE DATES.
7. CHECK THE EVIDENCE.
8. LOOK AT OTHER REPORTS.
9. IS THE STORY A JOKE?
10. SOME STORIES ARE INTENTIONALLY FALSE.

Although many of these ideas have already been covered in this book, seeing the ideas coming from Facebook may lend a deeper sense of urgency and importance for your students. Also, repeated exposure to these ideas can only help to reinforce their importance in fighting fake news.

To help students to personalize this information and to transition them from consumers to producers, challenge them to create a graphic to post on Facebook or other social media using Canva (https://www.canva.com) or a similar graphic design tool. Canva offers a large number of templates for square designs that are often shared on social media platforms such as Facebook and Instagram. Canva also offers access to a library of millions of images to use for free.

Rather than attempting to create a graphic with all 10 tips, ask students to tackle only one at a time. This will allow for a more focused effort on the importance of each item. Push students to create images that are impactful and memorable. Also, do not feel that you have to be limited to only using Canva and its templates. Instead encourage your students to tell their stories. Finally, remember that their work should be shared widely. Have students post their creations to a variety of social media platforms using the hashtag #FightingFakeNews. For more information and to see examples that I have collected, be sure to visit http://brianhousand.com/fakenews.

TWITTER

Although Facebook is at least attempting to take on some of the challenges that we face with regard to fake news, Twitter, on the other hand, is essentially the Wild West, where anyone can share anything that he or she wants. Unlike Facebook, which is a social network built primarily around friends and family, Twitter seeks to allow connections between anyone or anything through a brief post of up to 280 characters per tweet.

One of the major issues with Twitter and other social networks is that anyone can create an account and pretend to be someone that they are not. To further complicate matters, researchers from Indiana University and the University of Southern California estimated that between 9% and 15% of active Twitter accounts are bots (Varol, Ferrara, Davis, Menczer, & Flammini, 2017). These "bots" are automated software programs that can be programmed to periodically post messages to Twitter and are designed to seem like they are human. By utilizing bots, programmers can post similar messages from different accounts to make it seem like there is great interest in a particular topic when in fact it is only one person controlling hundreds of accounts simultaneously.

Twitter also allows for users to create accounts that may have very similar names. Take, for example, the image in Figure 15. There we see five different Twitter accounts purporting to be that of Donald Trump. However, only one of them serves as his official account. Try presenting the image to your students to see if they can clearly identify which one is the correct one and explain how they know.

The first Twitter account is that of @realDonaldTrump. We should note that there is a blue verified badge next to his name. Twitter provides these badges to let people know that an account of public interest is indeed authentic. This badge is always Twitter blue and is always placed in the same location in the profile. This is a good indication that the person or group behind the account is who they say that they are.

The second profile is from @RealTrump2016. Many times, you will see the use of the term "real" as an attempt to distinguish oneself from imposters. It is questionable whether or not this is account is real or not despite having nearly 45,000

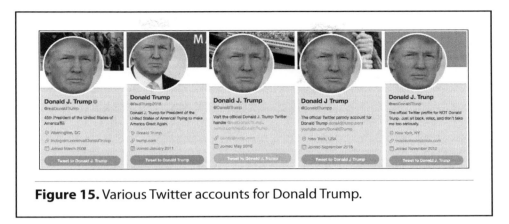

Figure 15. Various Twitter accounts for Donald Trump.

followers. However, this number pales in comparison to the more than 45 million followers @realDonalTrump has.

The third profile for @DonaldTrump serves as an attempt to grab hold of the Twitter handle that would seem to make the most sense. With more than 100,000 followers, this account has posted only one tweet, which instructs you to follow @realDonaldTrump.

The fourth (@DonaldTrumpp) and fifth (@realDonaldTrunp) profiles pictured offer examples of the importance of spelling. Each account is a parody, which is indicated in the profiles. However, when scrolling through a Twitter feed, it may be difficult to discern whether or not an account is real.

To better determine whether or not an account is real or fake, start with these four general pieces of advice.

1. **Check the spelling of the name.** Including a misspelling is a very common way to create a fake account.
2. **Read the profile.** Before believing a tweet or even retweeting, take a moment to click the account name and view the profile. Look for clues that would indicate that it is not a profile to be trusted.
3. **Look at who follows the account.** It has been said, "Show me who your friends are and I will show you who you are." This same strategy can be used for Twitter. Look to see who the account is are following and who is following it.
4. **Check for the Verification badge.** This is really the one safeguard that Twitter has put in place to clearly show that someone is who he or she says. However, Twitter also points out that just because an account has been verified does not necessarily indicate that Twitter supports the views that are expressed.

These four tips are a good place to start, but remember that the same set of strategies that we used in the Credentials stage of the CAPES framework on pages 63–64 could be utilized to cast a critical eye on Twitter accounts.

IMAGES

Although Twitter and Facebook were once heavily text-based, the rise of photo and video sharing sites like Instagram and Snapchat have had a huge influence on other social media platforms. If your social media feeds are anything like mine, then almost every post seems to have an accompanying photo with it. Perhaps this is because we have all heard that a picture is worth a thousand words, and when you are limited to 280 characters, a photo goes a long way.

Photos are also a good way to spread fake news. Although we may be quick to believe what we see with our own eyes, wherever you might find images, then you need to proceed with a skeptical eye. Thanks to access to a wide variety of photo editing tools, creating a fake photo is not as hard as it used to be.

To verify the authenticity of a photo and to learn more about the source of an image, teach your students to conduct a reverse image search using Google Images (https://images.google.com). There are two ways that this can be accomplished: (1) by uploading an image or screenshot, or (2) by searching for an online image with a URL.

Upload an Image

This works well if you already have an image on your computer or you have taken a screenshot of the image in question.
1. On https://images.google.com, click the camera icon to **Search by image**.
2. Click **Upload an image**.
3. Click **Choose file**.
4. Select the image from your computer.

Search Using an Image URL

1. On any website, right click on an image and select **Copy image address** or **Copy image location**.
2. On https://images.google.com or any Images results page, click the camera icon to **Search by image**.
3. Click **Paste image URL**.
4. Paste the URL you copied into the box.
5. Click **Search by image**.

The search results will display other sites for which the same image has been used before. This will help you to identify whether the image is original or has been altered in some way. Although Google Images may satisfy your needs for photo verification in most cases, it is always a good idea to double check your sources.

TinEye (https://www.tineye.com) provides an alternative to relying solely on a single source of information.

To put this new skill to the test, share Activity 13 (p. 112) with your students. Here you will find a tweet posted by @Jeggit on August 28, 2017, during Hurricane Harvey. The tweet includes a photo of a shark that appears to be swimming on a freeway in Houston. The text of the tweet reads, "Believe it or not, this is a shark on the freeway in Houston, Texas #HurricaneHarvey." Because of the sensational nature of the tweet, it was favorited and retweeted thousands of times.

According to a report in *The Washington Post*, news of this shark swimming on the highway was reported as real news by a Fox News anchor. Rather than being skeptical of such a report and checking his sources, the anchor was quick to share this sensationalized and fake news story. You can read all about this exchange and see a video clip of the news broadcast at https://www.washingtonpost.com/news/the-intersect/wp/2017/08/28/no-the-shark-picture-isnt-real-a-running-list-of-harveys-viral-hoaxes.

If the Fox News anchor had conducted a reverse image search, he would have realized that this photo is a hoax and has been previously used numerous times during other floods and hurricanes.

The anchor could have also taken the time to view the Twitter profile for @Jeggit. He would have learned that this is the Twitter account for Jason Michael, a Scottish journalist and blogger based in Dublin who writes on politics and society. He is a columnist for *iScot Magazine* and author of the Random Public Journal at https://randompublicjournal.com. Following any of these threads, one would have more than an ounce of suspicion regarding the authenticity of this supposed report of a shark sighting in Houston, TX.

CHAPTER 7:
ACTIVITIES AND HANDOUTS

SPOTTING FAKE NEWS

To help its users better identify false news, Facebook put together 10 suggestions for spotting false news.

1. BE SKEPTICAL OF HEADLINES.

2. LOOK CLOSELY AT THE URL.

3. INVESTIGATE THE SOURCE.

4. WATCH FOR UNUSUAL FORMATTING.

5. CONSIDER THE PHOTOS.

6. INSPECT THE DATES.

7. CHECK THE EVIDENCE.

8. LOOK AT OTHER REPORTS.

9. IS THE STORY A JOKE?

10. SOME STORIES ARE INTENTIONALLY FALSE.

Note. Adapted from Facebook, n.d.

ACTIVITY 13

JAWS!

Directions: View the tweet below, then answer the question related to this piece of shared media.

The following tweet appears in your Twitter feed:

ACTIVITY 13, CONTINUED.

What are three things that you could do to determine whether or not this actually happened?

1.

2.

3.

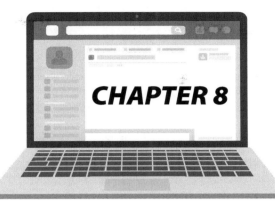

CHAPTER 8

OVERCOMING YOUR OWN BIAS

When you set out on the quest to fight fake news with me, we identified four challenges that we must overcome in this digital information age. We were first confronted with the challenge of *Information Overload*. To combat this, we focused on identifying important questions and locating information in Chapters 3 and 4. Next we faced the *Crisis of Authenticity,* and we equipped ourselves with CAPES in Chapter 5 to develop the power of critically evaluating information. To overcome the challenge of *Speed Versus Accuracy* we practiced searching for answers with multistep search problems and learned to synthesize information in Chapter 6 by building connections with Wikipedia Golf. However, we have yet to address the fourth challenge, and it may the most important one to address: *Overcoming Your Own Bias.*

As we use the Internet and other social media apps, our search habits are being mined to create a customized and personalized experience for us. The more that we use Google, the more that it learns about our interests. The more that we use Facebook and Twitter, the more that the advertisements and news we are presented with are tailored to our past practices. Although this level of personalization does have its advantages, it also comes at a cost. We are unknowingly being marketed to and potentially shutting ourselves off from multiple perspectives and opposing viewpoints.

During the 2016 presidential election, we visibly saw that not everyone in the U.S. necessarily thinks the same way that we do. Thanks in part to my Facebook feed, I learned that many of my friends and family had very different political viewpoints that I did. It was a real wake-up call, and on the evening of the 2016 presidential election, we saw very clearly the nation was almost evenly divided in its support for each of the candidates.

Although the Internet does offer access to almost infinite amounts of information, we are most likely to surround ourselves with like-minded people and interact with sources of information that only support our worldview. Rather than being a great equalizer of information, we have allowed the Internet to isolate us from opposing viewpoints. In many ways, the Internet and social media serve as an echo chamber that intensifies the volume of information that aligns with our beliefs while muting other perspectives.

The Importance of Multiple Perspectives

The National Council for the Social Studies (NCSS) developed a set of National Curriculum Standards for Social Studies centered around 10 themes (https://www. socialstudies.org/standards/strands). Prevalent throughout the standards is the idea that "in a multicultural, democratic society and globally connected world, students need to understand the multiple perspectives that derive from different cultural vantage points" (para. 1). If we desire to develop students capable of being competitive on a global level, then we must strive to teach them to see more than one perspective. As we have heard before, there are two sides to every coin.

In *Star Wars: Episode VI—Return of the Jedi* (Kazanijian & Marquand, 1983), Luke Skywalker returns to the planet Dagobah to complete his Jedi training. Still reeling from learning that Darth Vader is his father, he confronts Obi-Wan Kenobi, who had told him that Vader had betrayed and murdered his father. Obi-Wan explains that the man who had been his father ceased to exist when he turned to the dark side. In the following exchange, Obi-Wan goes on to explain to Luke how what we view as the truth depends on own perspective.

> **Obi-Wan:** "So what I told you was true, from a certain point of view."
> **Luke:** "A certain point of view?"
> **Obi-Wan:** "Luke, you're going to find that many of the truths we cling to depend greatly on our own point of view."

Obi-Wan Kenobi offers Luke some incredibly wise words to consider on the nature and permanence of what we believe the truth to be. Part of the learning process is questioning what our beliefs are and being able to support our beliefs with evidence.

Stepping Outside of Your Own Silo With AllSides

One way to better understand our beliefs and ourselves is to try looking at a news story from a different point of view. AllSides (https://www.allsides.com)

offers a balanced approach to today's news by presenting information from the left, right, and center points of view. The mission of AllSides (2018) is to "free people from filter bubbles so they can better understand the world and each other" (para. 1). It seeks to promote civil discourse among informed citizens.

In the example in Figure 16, we see a featured news story from December 29, 2017, where President Trump tweeted that the East Coast "could use a little bit of that good old Global Warming" to provide some relief from the frigid winter temperatures forecast for New Year's Eve. AllSides offers news stories from three different perspectives regarding the tweet. From the Right, TheBlaze reported that Trump mocks so-called "global warming" and that a Democrat doesn't like that one bit. From the Left, Vox posted "Trump thinks climate change isn't real because it's cold out. This map proves him wrong." CNN represents a view on the story from the center. Clicking on any one of the headlines will direct you to the full story online, where you and your students can read the details for yourself.

AllSides is very transparent about the bias rating of each of the news sources that it pulls from. A full list of the sources and their ratings is available at https://www.allsides.com/media-bias/media-bias-ratings. Users also have the ability to agree or disagree with the ratings. Also, AllSides continually monitors its ratings and adjusts them when necessary. For example, CNN is a highly contested source. As of this writing, AllSides classifies the CNN website as center. However, it does note that the CNN broadcast channel varies based on the news anchor and program and tends to lean left.

AllSides is very forthcoming with its own bias and rating system, and it encourages users to determine their own bias as well. To assist in this matter, AllSides offers a collection of online rating scales and surveys for you to utilize at https://www.allsides.com/rate-own-bias. Depending on the age and awareness level, the tools here may or may not be useful for your students. Be sure to preview each of these tools before using them.

Using AllSides in the Classroom

Start by selecting an appropriate topic for your students to investigate from the AllSides Topics and Issues page (https://www.allsides.com/topics-issues). Only you know best what is and is not appropriate for your students to discuss. Next, choose at least one news story from the left, center, and right. Present the three news stories to your students, but do not tell them the AllSides Bias Rating. Have them read and review each of the stories and then categorize them according to what they believe the bias is.

Figure 16. An example from AllSides. Screenshot from https://www.allsides.com/story/trump-tweets-about-global-warming.

From Consumer to Producer: Collecting Multiple Perspectives

At The Second Nelson Mandela Annual Lecture Address on May 23, 2004, Desmond Tutu shared a piece of advice his father gave him, "Don't raise your voice; improve your argument." It is all too tempting to let our emotions get the best of us when debating opposing views. Instead, it is better to take the time to consider our opposition's argument and examine its logic for flaws.

After your students have had some practice with examining news articles that you provide to them from AllSides, challenge them to locate sources of information that represent multiple viewpoints on a debatable topic that you select. Craft a brief position statement for your students to prompt their thinking—this will serve to focus the attention of you students, and you will avoid the problem of simply asking students to go online to conduct some Internet research.

Activity 14 (p. 121) provides a template to guide your students' thinking in the process. They should search for sources of information that are in support of and against the provided position statement you've written (students could also practice writing their own position statements with this template). While searching, they should also be on the lookout for sources that provide a balanced or neutral view on the topic. This is also a great time to go back and review the information related to the author's credentials that we covered as part of the CAPES framework in Chapter 5.

After students have gathered information from multiple perspectives, have them engage in some civil discourse around the topic. By this point, they should have a much clearer understanding of the issues from both sides. For an extra challenge, have students argue for an opposing viewpoint on a topic.

At this point, we have addressed four major challenges of the digital information age and learned some strategies for being more critical consumers of the information that we encounter. Now is the time to take on one final challenge. Are you ready to go head to head with fake news?

CHAPTER 8:
ACTIVITIES AND HANDOUTS

COLLECTING MULTIPLE PERSPECTIVES

My father used to say, "Don't raise your voice; improve your argument".—Desmond Tutu

Directions:

1. Start with a debatable topic and write a position statement in the TOPIC box, or write the position statement provided by your teacher.

2. Next, locate at least one source of information that supports the stated position and summarize it in the PROS box.

3. Then, locate at least one source of information that is against the stated position and summarize it in the CONS box.

4. Finally, locate at least one source of information that represents a neutral position and summarize it in the NEUTRAL box.

ACTIVITY 14, CONTINUED.

TOPIC

PRO

CON

NEUTRAL

CHAPTER 9

THE BOSS BATTLE:
FIGHTING FAKE NEWS!

This is it! The time has come. We are now ready to go head to head with fake news. As a video game player, I think of this chapter as "The Boss Battle." For those of you who have no idea what I am talking about right now, let me explain. A boss in a video game is an especially challenging enemy that represents the end of a level or a game. The boss often puts all of your previously learned skills to the test and requires you to also try out some new strategies as well. In a boss battle, the boss will throw everything it has at you to try and defeat you. It is only by using patience and employing all that you have learned that you will be able to overcome the boss and ultimately win the game.

For this penultimate chapter, we will proceed through six rounds in our final fight against fake news:

- Round One: Proceed With Caution! Clickbait Chum Box
- Round Two: Google the Headline
- Round Three: Read the Whole Article
- Round Four: Check the Facts
- Round Five: Use Common Sense
- Round Six: When In Doubt, Don't Share!

With each new round, we will face a new challenge to overcome.

ROUND ONE: PROCEED WITH CAUTION! CLICKBAIT CHUM BOX

In the film, *Star Wars: Episode IV—A New Hope* (Kurtz & Lucas, 1977), just before entering Mos Eisley Spaceport, Obi-Wan Kenobi advised that "You will never find a more wretched hive of scum and villainy. We must be cautious." The same could be said for what I like to think of as the clickbait chum box. You have undoubtedly seen clickbait before, and you have probably even clicked on more items than you would care to admit. Chum is bait consisting of mostly inedible fish parts, blood, and bone. Chum is often thrown in the water to attract larger fish, particularly sharks. Clickbait usually lives at the bottom of a webpage and is contained in a box like the one in Figure 17.

The sole purpose of the clickbait chum box is to entice you to click on one of the scintillating headlines to visit an external site that is typically filled with advertising, mindless surveys, or lists of lists. Clickbait is generated by an ever-growing number of purveyors such as ZergNet, OutBrain, and Taboola, and it is often used host to fake news and other general unpleasantries.

Clickbait headlines are constructed in such a way as to pique your curiosity and evoke an emotional response. They are designed to give you just enough information to make you wonder what else could possibly be revealed if you just clicked. They provide you with very little about the actual content of the article. Clickbait is often accompanied by a photo that may have little relation to the actual story and is intended to capture your attention. Figure 18 includes the eight most common clickbait traps you can share with your students or post in your classroom.

From Consumer to Producer: Create Clickbait for a Historical Event

To defeat the challenge of the clickbait chum box, we are going to try and beat the Fake News Boss at its own game. Have your students create a list of potential clickbait headlines for a historical event.

For example, a clickbait headline for the assassination of Abraham Lincoln might read "This man went to see a play, and what happened next blew his mind!" A story about Rosa Parks might have the clickbait headline, "I never thought riding the bus would make me so angry." "Two bicycle repairmen in Kitty Hawk will change the way you think about travel" could be a clickbait headline for a story about Orville and Wilbur Wright.

To get started, begin by providing an historical event or time period for your students. This will help them to focus their creative energies. Next, in small groups have them brainstorm with at least 10 separate headlines. Then, have the groups share their headlines with the class to see which ones are the most compelling and would potentially garner the most clicks.

Figure 17. Example of a clickbait chum box.

Finally, have students create a PowerPoint slide, meme, or social media post that includes an image to accompany the clickbait headline.

Encourage your students to post their creations on social media using the hashtags #FightingFakeNews #HistoricalClickbait. I will be collecting my favorites and posting them on my website at http://brianhousand.com/fakenews.

By having students construct their own clickbait, the hope is that they will be more aware of clickbait when they see it, and if they do click on it, that they will proceed with caution and skepticism before simply believing everything that they read.

ROUND TWO: GOOGLE THE HEADLINE

As we just saw with clickbait, a compelling headline can drive us toward a website like a moth to a flame. Sites that spread fake news often try to create the most sensational headline possible to attract more readers. For example, *The Onion* (https://www.theonion.com), an openly satirical news organization, is masterful at creating such headlines. Yet, many times stories from *The Onion* get retweeted or shared on Facebook as real news based solely on the headline. To fight the Fake News Boss, a simple strategy is to google the headline before believing or sharing the story. A simple copy and paste into your favorite search engine can provide valuable insight into the authenticity of the news story.

EIGHT CLICKBAIT TRAPS AND HOW THEY FOOL YOU EVERY TIME!

1. **YOU WILL NEVER GUESS WHY!** This draws you in by challenging your intelligence. You want to click on this headline because you want to prove how smart you are.

2. **WHAT WE FOUND WAS SHOCKING!** Humans are naturally curious and we will willingly click on a headline if we think that we can learn something potentially unbelievable or bizarre. This is precisely the psychology that was utilized by franchises like *Ripley's Believe It or Not!* and even *America's Got Talent.*

3. **11 THINGS THAT YOU PROBABLY DID NOT KNOW ABOUT YOUR FAVORITE CELEBRITY.** This item combines two strategies together: lists and celebrities. There is just something utterly compelling about a numbered list. Did you notice that I lured you in with the promise of eight clickbait traps? Also, humans seem to be hungry for information about the lives of celebrities. Just take a look at the tabloid magazines in any grocery store checkout lane.

4. **BEST NEW TECH TOOLS! NUMBER 4 IS MY FAVORITE!** This is another twist on the numbered list, but it compels you to keep reading until you get to the number that has been identified even if you have already grown tired of reading and clicking.

5. **WHAT EVERY SUCCESSFUL PERSON MUST KNOW.** Clickbait like this promises to offer some sage advice or wisdom to those willing to click. By not clicking this headline, you are saying that you do not want to be successful.

6. **FEEL BETTER ABOUT YOURSELF BY DOING THIS.** There is often the promise of some type of health or psychological benefit by doing something that is very simple.

7. **LOSE WEIGHT NOW BY EATING THESE FOODS.** A large number of clickbait headlines target those who are looking to easily lose weight without any real effort.

8. **HOW TO SAVE $$$ ON YOUR NEXT PURCHASE.** Who does not want to save money? Also, related to this would be anything related to quickly earning money with little or no work.

Figure 18. Eight clickbait traps.

ROUND THREE: READ THE WHOLE ARTICLE

OK, I will admit it. There have been more than a few times that I have shared something on Twitter when I did not read the entire article. Instead, I skimmed through it to get the general gist of the article and felt that others should see it as well. Thankfully, this Fake News Boss has never defeated me, but as I have been writing this book, I have become much more conscientious about what I am willing to share online. Caution your students to be sure to completely read something before sharing it as truth.

ROUND FOUR: CHECK THE FACTS

After actually reading an article, you may still be in doubt regarding the authenticity of the information. The Fake News Boss can be very convincing and will fool even some of your best students. According to the 2017 report *News and America's Kids* from Common Sense Media, only 44% of children agree that they know how to tell fake news stories from real ones. Meanwhile 31% of those surveyed had shared a news story online that they later found out was wrong or inaccurate and 28% were unsure if they had done so or not (Robb, 2017).

One of the best defenses against the Fake News Boss in this instance is to use one or more of the available fact-checking sites to verify the authenticity of the news story. Some of the best of these include:

- **PolitiFact—http://www.politifact.com:** A project of the *Tampa Bay Times*, PolitiFact is a nonpartisan fact-checking website that focuses on American politics and rates the accuracy of claims by elected officials using a system that it calls the Truth-O-Meter. This metric offers ratings of True, Mostly True, Half True, Mostly False, False, and Pants on Fire! PolitiFact selects newsworthy claims and utilizes journalistic principles to deeply investigate its stories before publishing. Winner of the Pulitzer Prize for National Reporting in 2009, PolitiFact is widely considered to an accurate political fact checker. However, there is some criticism that PolitiFact may lean left. Like Snopes, PolitiFact relies on advertising for support, although there are far fewer ads on each page.
- **FactCheck.org—https://www.factcheck.org:** A project of the Annenberg Public Policy Center at the University of Pennsylvania, FactCheck.org (2018) describes itself as "a nonpartisan, non-profit 'consumer advocate' for voters that aims to reduce the level of deception and confusion in U.S. politics." Unlike Snopes and PoltiFact, FactCheck.org does not feature any type of advertising and is entirely funded by endowments from the Annenberg Foundation and the Flora Family Foundation. FactCheck.org primarily focuses on political news but does occasionally address inter-

net rumors (https://www.factcheck.org/hot-topics) and offers SciCheck (https://www.factcheck.org/scicheck) to fact check science-based claims.

- **Snopes—https://www.snopes.com:** What began in 1994 as an interest in folklore and urban myths has developed into one of the most widely utilized sites for determining fact from fiction on the Internet. Snopes is a great first checkpoint for your students. The site offers a search box for easy access to precisely the topic that you are looking for. Snopes offers a clear and easy to understand rating system (https://www.snopes.com/ratings). One real downside to the Snopes website is the amount of advertising on its pages. Other than that, Snopes does offer a detailed description of its background checking process for every claim that it investigates.

Although fact-checking sites like the ones mentioned here can provide a line of defense against fake news, they are not entirely foolproof and, like all sources of information, must be utilized with a healthy dose of skepticism. In an entry entitled "False Authority" (https://www.snopes.com/lost/false.asp), Snopes founder David Mikkelson (2017) provided some straightforward advice.

> No single truth purveyor, no matter how reliable, should be considered an infallible font of accurate information. Folks make mistakes. Or they get duped. Or they have a bad day at the fact-checking bureau. Or some days they're just being silly. To not allow for any of this is to risk stepping into a pothole the size of Lake Superior. (para. 9)

Perhaps the only truth of the matter is that everyone makes mistakes. We have to be cautious and skeptical at all times and of all things. We cannot outsource our critical thinking and fact-checking to others without also checking their facts, or as Mikkelson (2017) stated, "Common sense dictates that you should never fully rely upon someone else to do fact checking for you. But who has time for common sense?" (para. 1).

ROUND FIVE: USE COMMON SENSE

Perhaps the best defense of all against the Fake News Boss is just using our own common sense. For our students who have yet to develop a informed and broad view of the world, this may be particularly difficult. Throughout this book, I have sought to provide you with some tools and strategies to help better equip you and your students with a critical mind. However, perhaps the simplest strategy to adopt is one that you have probably already taught them: asking questions using the 5Ws and 1H.

Posing questions related to Who, What, When, Where Why, and How is the toolbox of every great journalist and inquiring mind. To better focus these very general questions, I have developed Activity 15 (p. 133) for you to share with your students. Begin by providing them with a link to a website or news story. This may or may not be an item of fake news. Have them adopt the mind of a detective and investigate the provided resource using the questions provided. Then, as a class, have students determine whether or not this is a reliable source of information.

ROUND SIX: WHEN IN DOUBT, DON'T SHARE!

"A lie can travel half way around the world while the truth is putting on its shoes." This quote is often attributed to Mark Twain, but ironically there is very little evidence to suggest he ever actually said or wrote this. In this digital age with instant access to information, what is shared online has the potential to reach a global audience in the blink of an eye. Maybe the easiest way to defeat the Fake New Boss is to remember this: When in doubt about the authenticity of information, simply do not share it with others. Although you may jokingly post something that you know to be untrue, your friends and followers might not be as savvy or as cautious as you are.

By sharing these final six strategies with your students, you can effectively empower them to face many of the challenges that fake news might throw at them. As with the CAPES Framework in Chapter 5, I encourage you to challenge your students to create digital posters with each of these six recommendations and share them on social media. This will further empower your students and help others to battle the Fake News Boss. Be sure to use the hashtags #FightingFakeNews and #FakeNewsBossBattle. I will be collecting some of the best examples and posting them on my website at http://brianhousand.com/fakenews.

CHAPTER 9:
ACTIVITIES AND HANDOUTS

Name: _____ Date: _____

FIGHTING FAKE NEWS WITH 5WS AND 1H

Directions: Using the news story provided by your teacher, investigate the information included using the 5Ws and 1H.

	ASK YOURSELF	RECORD YOUR THINKING
WHO?	Who is saying this? Look for an ABOUT page to let you know what makes them an expert.	
WHAT?	What is being said? Is the information factual?	
WHEN?	When was the information posted? Is the information up to date? Does it need to be up to date?	
WHERE?	Where did you find the information? Did you find it yourself or was it shared by someone else?	
WHY?	Why is the information being posted? Is it reporting news, entertainment, selling something, or for humor?	
HOW?	How does the information make you feel? Is it meant to evoke an emotional response?	

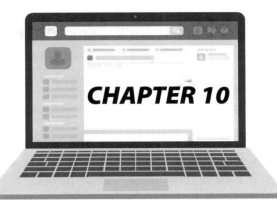

CHAPTER 10

EPILOGUE:
PAY ATTENTION

Several years ago, my wife, Angela, and I visited the Holocaust Museum in Washington, DC. Near the beginning of the main exhibit, there is a section that powerfully presents how propaganda was subtly introduced by the Nazi party in Germany. In the beginning, the messages did not seem to be that out of the ordinary, but as they continued, they managed to slowly seep into the collective conscious of many who would go on to do horrible things during the Holocaust.

Early this year over dinner, Angela and I were discussing how the rise of fake news and its spread feels in many ways like it is echoing much of what we saw in that part of the exhibit in the museum. My intent here is not to suggest that we are on the brink of a similar humanitarian disaster. Instead, my intent is to say that if we do not pay attention and stand up for what we believe in, then many of the freedoms that we take for granted may be stripped away from us.

As I have been writing this book, I was reminded of all of the great curriculum that has been developed related to the subject of propaganda. I can remember very vividly learning from my middle school gifted teacher about different propaganda techniques and how advertising can provide the power of suggestion without anyone realizing it. As a teacher, I loved sharing with my students similar activities. In the age of fake news, it is time to dust off those units that you may have been holding on to for a while and breathe new life into them. My hope is that this book will give you new material to supplement what may have already been very effective curriculum.

In early 2017, George Orwell's novel *1984* became a *New York Times* bestselling novel. This book, written nearly 70 years ago about a dystopian future, suddenly seemed more relevant than ever before. Many point to an interview that appeared on NBC's *Meet The Press* with Kellyanne Conway as the impetus for the rise in book sales. In the interview, Conway defended a claim made by then White House press secretary, Sean Spicer, that the inauguration of President Trump was the largest ever to assemble, and she said that Mr. Spicer "gave alternative facts." Use of this term raised the hackles of the American public and drew obvious comparisons to terms like *newspeak* and *doublethink* in Orwell's novel.

Although fears that we are entering a world similar to *1984* may be hyperbolic, what is important is that we wake up and pay attention to what is going on in the world around us. Although the 2016 presidential election cast a glaring light on the difference of opinions and beliefs in our country, I have been impressed by the raised consciousness of large numbers of individuals who may not previously have considered themselves political becoming increasingly involved in the democratic process. If fake news and alternative facts have been a part of this wake up call, then perhaps this is not an entirely bad thing after all. That being said, there is a great deal of work that lies ahead for us. To conclude this book, I would like to end with three final pieces of advice for you and your students.

1. SAYING SOMETHING IS REAL DOES NOT MAKE IT REAL, AND SAYING SOMETHING IS FAKE DOES NOT MAKE IT FAKE

As much as I would like for aliens and unicorns to be real, there is simply not enough substantial evidence at this point in time to prove their existence. Saying that aliens or unicorns are real does not make them real. Likewise, saying something is fake does not make it fake. There have been a multitude of claims by President Donald Trump and many others that news and events that are verifiable are #FakeNews. Simply put, labeling something with a term or a hashtag does not make it so. We have to cautiously approach such boisterous claims of falsehood in the same way that we might approach the boy who cried wolf.

2. TRUST, BUT VERIFY

If I have learned anything in the process of writing this book, then it is that there is very little that is beyond the shadow of doubt. Instead, we must shine the bright light of skepticism on all information. However, living life in this matter can become quite exhausting, and certainly, we all have sources of information that we want to believe are reliable. Therefore, I propose that we adopt the saying "trust, but verify" as part of our interactions with the news. This phrase was one that was used by President Ronald Reagan many times during the nuclear disarmament negotiations with the Soviet Union, and it provides a way forward for us in the age of fake news. We seek verification from additional sources whenever possible.

3. DON'T BE A KNOW-IT-ALL— DO BE A LEARN-IT-ALL

It is impossible to know absolutely everything. Yet, many of our students pride themselves on striving to be a "know-it-all," and in many ways schools have set this up as a something that is humanly possible. When bright students are constantly praised for being "perfect" and easily earn 100% on every assignment they encounter, then we are setting them up for failure in the future. At some point, they are going to encounter a task that they cannot overcome, and then they are going to doubt that they were ever smart. In the age of the Internet, it is possible to learn how to do almost anything. Google is perhaps the most powerful how-to book that has ever existed. With a quick search, websites, YouTube videos, and multiple tutorials can guide you to the information that you are looking for. Instead of praising your students for what it is that they already know, let's focus on praising them for the ability to learn something new. The ability to learn, to discover, to question, and to find truth is what will ultimately win the war against fake news.

ADDITIONAL RESOURCES

One of the great challenges of writing this book was that I was trying to hit a moving target. Barely a week went by when I did not find a new resource or report on the topic of fake news. With every new piece of information, I found myself shifting my focus. To be quite honest, I felt a little bit like a squirrel running around trying to make sense of this important but elusive topic. Throughout my work, I bookmarked several resources that did not necessarily find their way into this book. However, I feel that a great deal of what was left on the cutting room floor is well worth your time for further investigation. What I offer here is a link to some of my legwork in the process.

AllSides for Schools
https://www.allsides.com/schools

This site provides resources to help educators facilitate classroom discussions involving current events and controversial topics while avoiding bias and serious divisions in the classroom. Lessons focus on teaching critical thinking, collaboration, listening with respect, as well as digital literacy and social-emotional learning. Issue lesson plans cover topics such as immigration, climate change, and the wage gap. Another highlight is the Dictionary Term Lesson Plan, which uses potentially hot topics as a mean of teaching about differences in opinion and perspective.

Checkology
https://checkology.org

From the News Literacy Project, Checkology features a set of core lessons to help equip students with tools to evaluate and interpret the news. The platform features a free basic access and a premium subscription service that allows you to monitor student work on the lessons. Journalists, digital media experts, and First Amendment scholars guide students though a series of online interactive lessons.

News and America's Kids: How Young People Perceive and Are Impacted by the News **by Common Sense**
**https://www.commonsensemedia.org/sites/default/files/uploads/research/
2017_commonsense_newsandamericaskids.pdf**

Eye-opening data regarding how today's youth and the news media interact are presented in this research monograph from Common Sense Media. The free publication features a large number of interesting charts and graphs, as well as an excellent infographic that summarizes the key findings from the report that would serve as an excellent discussion starter for you and your students. The page for the infographic is not numbered in the report, but it immediately follows the Table of Contents and is located on page 5 of the PDF.

"How to Spot Fake News" by FactCheck.Org
https://www.factcheck.org/2016/11/how-to-spot-fake-news

In this article from FactCheck.Org, many common-sense strategies for spotting fake news are presented, including reading beyond the headline, checking the date, and asking important questions, such as "Is this some kind of joke?"

"How to Spot Fake News Poster" by International Federation of Library Associations and Institutions
https://www.ifla.org/publications/node/11174

This is an infographic that presents eight strategies for spotting fake news that is available for download as a PDF or JPG file. The information has also been translated into more than 30 different languages. This is a great source of inspiration for you and your students as you design you own posters and infographics to help spread the word on ways to fight fake news.

Newseum ED
https://newseumed.org/ed-tools

ED Tools from the Newseum, a museum dedicated to the history of news media located in Washington, DC, presents an ever-growing collection of standards-aligned lesson plans, artifacts, and case studies. This link features multiple activities related to the topic of fake news. Some of my personal favorites include "Is This Story Shareworthy?" (https://newseumed.org/activity/is-this-story-shareworthy-flowchart-mlbp) and "E.S.C.A.P.E. Junk News" (https://newseumed.org/activity/e-s-c-a-p-e-junk-news-mlbp). You do have to register for a free educator account to access all of the materials.

"Evaluating Sources in a 'Post-Truth' World: Ideas for Teaching and Learning About Fake News" by *The New York Times*
https://www.nytimes.com/2017/01/19/learning/lesson-plans/evaluating-sources-in-a-post-truth-world-ideas-for-teaching-and-learning-about-fake-news.html

This is a collection of lesson ideas from various sources curated by *The New York Times*. Some of the ideas are summaries from other sources in this list and throughout this book. That being said, it does provide a number of previously unmentioned resources that serve as a good warehouse of lesson ideas for use with your students.

"Hoax or No Hoax? Strategies for Online Comprehension and Evaluation" by ReadWriteThink
http://www.readwritethink.org/classroom-resources/lesson-plans/hoax-hoax-strategies-online-1135.html

A project of the International Literacy Association and the National Council of Teachers of English, ReadWriteThink is an excellent resource for all things reading and writing. This link directs you to a set of lesson plans and extension activities designed for four 60-mintue sessions. Although intended for high school students, many of the ideas could be easily modified or scaffolded for use with younger students.

"Civic Online Reasoning" by Stanford History Education Group
https://sheg.stanford.edu/civic-online-reasoning

The team from the Stanford History Education Group (SHEG) have created a series of research-based activities targeted for students in middle grades, high school, and college designed to help better teach students to critically evaluate the flood of online information. The activities focus on evaluating information from specific platforms, including Wikipedia, YouTube, and Twitter. Other lessons teach students to compare articles, examine evidence, and analyze arguments. You can read more about the research and development of these activities in the report *Evaluating Information: The Cornerstone of Civic Online Reasoning* at https://purl.stanford.edu/fv751yt5934.

REFERENCES

AllSides. (2018). *The AllSides mission.* Retrieved from https://www.allsides.com/about

Anderson, L., & Krathwohl, D. R. (Eds.). (2001). *A taxonomy for learning, teaching, and assessing: A revision of Bloom's taxonomy of educational objectives* (Complete ed.). New York, NY: Longman.

Bloom, B., Englehart, M. Furst, E., Hill, W., & Krathwohl, D. (1956). *Taxonomy of educational objectives: The classification of educational goals. Handbook I: Cognitive domain.* New York, NY: Longmans, Green.

Coiro, J. (2007). *Exploring changes to reading comprehension on the Internet: Paradoxes and possibilities for diverse adolescent readers* (Unpublished doctoral dissertation). University of Connecticut, Storrs.

Facebook. (n.d.). *Tips to spot false news—Facebook help center.* Retrieved from https://www.facebook.com/help/188118808357379

Factcheck.org. (2018). *Our mission.* Retrieved from https://www.factcheck.org/about/our-mission

Harris, R. (2016). *Evaluating internet research sources.* Retrieved from https://www.virtualsalt.com/evalu8it.htm

Kazanijian, H. (Producer), & Marquand, R. (Director). (1983). *Star Wars: Episode VI—Return of the Jedi* [Motion picture]. United States: 20th Century Fox.

Kurtz, G. (Producer), & Lucas, G. (Director). (1977). *Star Wars: Episode IV—A New Hope* [Motion Picture]. United States: 20th Century Fox.

Leu, D. J. (2006). New literacies, reading research, and the challenges of change: A deictic perspective. In J. V. Hoffman, D. L. Schallert, C. M. Fairbanks, J. Worthy, & B. Maloch (Eds.), *55th Yearbook of the National Reading Conference* (pp. 1–20). Oak Creek, WI: National Reading Conference.

Leu, D. J., Zawilinski, L., Castek, J., Banerjee, M., Housand, B., Liu, Y., . . . Hartman, D. K. (2007). What is new about the new literacies of online reading comprehension? In L. Rush, J. Eakle, & A. Berger (Eds.), *Secondary school literacy: What research reveals for classroom practices* (pp. 37–68). Urbana, IL: National Council of Teachers of English.

Landsberg, A. (1977–1982). *In Search Of . . .* [Television Series]. Alan Landsberg Productions.

Meriam Library. (n.d.). *Is this source or information good?* Retrieved from http://library.csuchico.edu/help/source-or-information-good

Mikkelson, D. (2017). False authority. *Snopes.* Retrieved from https://www.snopes.com/lost/false.asp

Mosseri, A. (2017). *Working to stop misinformation and false news.* Retrieved from https://newsroom.fb.com/news/2017/04/working-to-stop-misinformation-and-false-news

National Council for the Social Studies. (n.d.). *National Curriculum Standards for Social Studies: Chapter 2–The themes of social studies.* Retrieved from https://www.socialstudies.org/standards/strands

Oxford Dictionaries. (2016). *Oxford Dictionaries Word of the Year 2016 is . . . post-truth.* Retrieved from https://www.oxforddictionaries.com/press/news/2016/12/11/WOTY-16

Pew Research Center. (2016). *News use across social media platforms 2016.* Retrieved from http://assets.pewresearch.org/wp-content/uploads/sites/13/2016/05/PJ_2016.05.26_social-media-and-news_FINAL-1.pdf

Pink, D. H. (2005). *A whole new mind: Why right-brainers will rule the future.* New York, NY: Riverhead Books.

Plutchik, R. (1980). A general psychoevolutionary theory of emotion. In R. Plutchik, & H. Kelleman (Eds.), *Emotion: Theory, research, and experience. Volume 1: Theories of emotion* (pp. 3–34). New York, NY: Academic Press.

Robb, M. B. (2017). *News and America's kids: How young people perceive and are impacted by the news.* San Francisco, CA: Common Sense.

Shirky, C. (2008). *It's not information overload. It's filter failure.* Presentation at Web 2.0 Expo, New York, NY.

Soll, J. (2016, December 18). The long and brutal history of fake news. *POLITICO Magazine.* Retrieved from http://www.politico.com/magazine/story/2016/12/fake-news-history-long-violent-214535

Taboada, A., & Guthrie, J. T. (2006). Contributions of student questioning and prior knowledge to construction of knowledge from reading information text. *Journal of Literacy Research, 38,* 1–35.

Toffler, A. (1970). *Future shock.* New York, NY: Random House.

Tzu, S. (1963). *The art of war* (S. B. Griffith, Trans.). New York, NY: Oxford University Press.

Varol, O., Ferrara, E., Davis, C. A., Menczer, F., & Flammini, A. (2017). *Online human-bot interactions: Detection, estimation, and characterization.* Retrieved from https://arxiv.org/abs/1703.03107

Wikipedia. (n.d.). *Yeti.* Retrieved from https://en.wikipedia.org/wiki/Yeti

Wolf, G. (1996, Feb.). Steve Jobs: The next insanely great thing. *Wired.* Retrieved from https://www.wired.com/1996/02/jobs-2

ABOUT THE AUTHOR

Brian C. Housand, Ph.D., is an associate professor and coordinator of the Academically and Intellectually Gifted Program at East Carolina University. Dr. Housand earned a Ph.D., in educational psychology at the University of Connecticut with an emphasis in both gifted education and instructional technology. He currently serves on the National Association for Gifted Children's Board of Directors as a Member-At-Large. Along with his wife, Dr. Angela Housand, and Dr. Joseph Renzulli, he coauthored *Using the Schoolwide Enrichment Model With Technology*. He researches ways in which technology can enhance the learning environment and is striving to define creative productive giftedness in a digital age. For more information, go to http://brianhousand.com.